The Global Future of
English Studies

Blackwell Manifestos

In this new series major critics make timely interventions to address important concepts and subjects, including topics as diverse as, for example: Culture, Race, Religion, History, Society, Geography, Literature, Literary Theory, Shakespeare, Cinema, and Modernism. Written accessibly and with verve and spirit, these books follow no uniform prescription but set out to engage and challenge the broadest range of readers, from undergraduates to postgraduates, university teachers and general readers – all those, in short, interested in ongoing debates and controversies in the humanities and social sciences.

Already Published

The Global Future of English Studies

James F. English

WILEY-BLACKWELL

A John Wiley & Sons, Ltd., Publication

This edition first published 2012
© 2012 John Wiley & Sons, Ltd

Wiley-Blackwell is an imprint of John Wiley & Sons, formed by the merger of Wiley's global Scientific, Technical and Medical business with Blackwell Publishing.

Registered Office
John Wiley & Sons Ltd, The Atrium, Southern Gate, Chichester, West Sussex, PO19 8SQ, UK

Editorial Offices
350 Main Street, Malden, MA 02148-5020, USA
9600 Garsington Road, Oxford, OX4 2DQ, UK
The Atrium, Southern Gate, Chichester, West Sussex, PO19 8SQ, UK

For details of our global editorial offices, for customer services, and for information about how to apply for permission to reuse the copyright material in this book please see our website at www.wiley.com/wiley-blackwell.

The right of James F. English to be identified as the author of this work has been asserted in accordance with the UK Copyright, Designs and Patents Act 1988.

Library of Congress Cataloging-in-Publication Data
English, James F., 1958–
    The global future of English studies / James F. English.
      p. cm.
    Includes index.
    ISBN 978-0-470-65494-1 (cloth)
    1. English language–Study and teaching.   I. Title.
    PE1065.E56 2012
    420.7–dc23

                          2011042251

A catalogue record for this book is available from the British Library.

Set in 11.5/13.5 pt Bembo by Toppan Best-set Premedia Limited
Printed and bound in Singapore by Markono Print Media Pte Ltd

1   2012

For Jimmy, John, and Eileen

Contents

Contents

List of Illustrations

List of Illustrations

Preface

This is not a prescriptive manifesto on method, calling for a new approach to research, a new theorization of the literary object, or a new form of pedagogical practice. There are always plenty of books in circulation announcing new programs of research and teaching; such books are indeed one of the great constants of our discipline, one of the products it most reliably produces – one of the signs, indeed, of its stability and vigor. Yet when we step back to take a long view of literary studies, even the most contentious debates over specific disciplinary assumptions and practices tend to appear as minor eruptions on a placid surface, affecting a relatively small number of faculty and graduate students who are housed in a few exceptional institutions. As Barbara Herrnstein Smith observed in the midst of the fierce conflicts of the early 1990s, when English faculty were accused of pursuing a wholesale assault on the discipline's traditional texts and values, "nothing in higher education has been more stable over the past 40 years than the curriculum of departments of English."

This is not to deny that important changes have taken place. Recent decades have witnessed seismic shifts on the global terrain of higher education and English has not escaped the disruption and turmoil. But the changes it has been undergoing are not of the sort that can be addressed in a standard-issue manifesto on critical method. The overabundance of English PhDs in Western Europe and North America and the acute shortage in many countries of South and East Asia; the explosion of creative writing programs throughout the Anglophone world; the widening effort, now evident in China, to reform the "English Plus" model and decouple English literary studies from the teaching of business writing and English for engineers: these kinds of changes are large scale − often too large scale for us even to register them in any coherent way, let alone to incorporate them into our disputes over theory and method. My aim here is to draw these kinds of tectonic shifts, and the tensions underlying them, into the compass of our more immediate matters of concern. To be sure, this widening of attention leads to certain implications for critical and pedagogical practice: that we should veer off from the orthodoxies of the (now almost elderly) "new" historicism; that we should adjust departmental formations, degree requirements, and standard coursework to emphasize the critical learning inherent in creative writing and the creative element in critical writing; that we should extend beyond the comfort zone of our habitual interdisciplinarities to form alliances with the quantitative social and informational sciences; and so on. But the purpose of this book is not so much to lay out my own agenda for English studies as to offer, however sketchily and imperfectly, the groundwork for clearer collective thinking about what the agenda should be. While I will maintain that our discipline's future is not nearly so bleak as most commentators imagine, it does face major challenges. And our success in meeting those challenges will depend, to begin with, on our ability to map the new global landscape on which we are operating.

Acknowledgments

I could not have written this book without assistance from faculty and students in various English departments around the world. My colleagues at Penn, especially Peter Conn and Max Cavitch, have been among my most thoughtful and well-informed interlocutors. During my time teaching at Kings College, London, I learned much about the specificities of the British system from conversations with Mark Turner, Jo McDonagh, and Gordon McMullan. When he was at the University of Edinburgh, John Frow engaged me in a project of administrative data exchange between the English departments there, at Penn, and at the University of Melbourne. Elizabeth Anderson performed heroic labor in assembling the Penn data for that study, the results of which proved helpful to this book in a number of ways. David Carter arranged for me to make an extended visit to the University of Queensland, where my sense of the situation of English departments in Australia was sharpened by conversations with Nathan Garvey, Roger Osborne, Ian Hunter, and David himself. I also learned much from the Australian and New Zealand scholars at the 2011 SHARP Conference in Brisbane, and especially from Simone Murray of Monash University, who, among other things, explained to me the "Melbourne model." Henrik Enbohm of the Swedish Writers'

Acknowledgments

Union invited me to a large gathering of writers, scholars, and translators in Stockholm, where I was able to speak with faculty and graduate students from literature departments in Sweden and elsewhere in Scandinavia. Andrew Shields at the University of Basel provided me with helpful information about English studies in Switzerland and Germany, as did Philipp Schweighauser and Ina Habermann. In Vienna, my Austrian guide was Hanno Biber, and I am grateful to Lianna Giorgi of the ICCR and the Euro-Festival Project for arranging my visit to that city, as well as to Bologna. Most recently, Rudolph Glitz arranged for me to visit the University of Amsterdam and provided clear and detailed answers to my queries regarding English studies in the Netherlands.

For helping me to learn something about English departments in China, I owe a particular debt to Danling Li, my tireless guide and native informant in Beijing, who has continued to assist me back in Philadelphia. Wang Ning arranged my visit to Tsinghua University and set up a series of meetings and meals there; Shen Anfeng gave me a most informative tour of the campus. Mao Liang arranged my visit to Peking University, where he, Ding Hongwei, Thomas Rendall, and Shen Dan all patiently answered my many questions about their students, curriculums, teaching methods, and funding arrangements. Zhang Hongxia was a charming and informative guide in Shanghai. Junsong Chen of Shanghai International Studies University led me on a most enlightening tour of the English literature section of the SISU bookstore. He Weiwen, vice dean of the School of Foreign Languages at Shanghai Jiaotong University, hosted me on his campus, where I enjoyed helpful discussions with him and Wang Zhenhua. Sun Jian, the chair of English at Fudan University, generously made time for me in the middle of a busy week. My visit to Nanjing University was especially productive, and Liu Haiping did me great service in arranging for meetings with groups of administrators, faculty, and graduate students. Especially helpful was the participation of Yang Jincai, the dean of the School of Foreign Studies, and Gao Wei, Zhu Gang, Zhao Wenshu, Zhu Xuefeng, Hu Jing, and Fan Hao. Finally, Phoebe Liu, my student at Penn, translated Chinese documents and websites for me, and canvassed her friends at universities in China for information that we could not find online.

No one has assisted me more with this book than David Dunning, who prepared all the charts and contributed much clarity of thought to the task of gathering and analyzing the statistical data. David also read the book in manuscript, steering me around numerous mistakes, as did the copyeditor Cheryl Adam at a later stage in the process. Fraser Sutherland worked rapidly to prepare an index. Aileen Castell was a superbly efficient project manager. Emma Bennett is the editor who originally encouraged me to write the book for her Manifesto series, and Ben Thatcher kept the project moving forward despite my habitual dodges, detours, and delays.

None of these people will fully agree with the analysis and arguments in the book. Nor do they share responsibility for whatever errors of fact and flaws of reasoning it contains. But the opportunity to discuss with them the present circumstances and possible futures of a discipline in which we are all invested has greatly enriched my understanding and enlivened my professional life these past few years.

Part I
The Future of English Enrollments
Massification and Global Demand

Beyond Crisis

For many readers of this book, particularly those who teach in US universities, it will come as strange news when I say that the academic discipline of English is not in a state of crisis, that its future actually looks pretty bright. Where have I been? Didn't I get the memo? A 2008 *Nation* magazine piece by Yale University's William Deresiewicz is more in sync with the professional pulse. "The number of students studying English literature," writes Deresiewicz, "appears to be in a steep, prolonged and apparently irreversible decline. In the past ten years, my department has gone from about 120 majors a year to about ninety a year. Fewer students mean fewer professors; during the same time, we've gone from about fifty-five full-time faculty positions to about forty-five. Student priorities are shifting to more 'practical' majors like economics." It really doesn't matter anymore where we may stand on questions of critical method, canon, or ideology, concludes Deresiewicz. The "real story of academic literary criticism today is that the profession is, however slowly, dying."[1]

The Global Future of English Studies, First Edition. James F. English.
© 2012 John Wiley & Sons, Ltd. Published 2012 by John Wiley & Sons, Ltd.

What makes Deresiewicz's diagnosis especially alarming is that he is writing from some of the highest and safest ground our field has to offer. This putative erosion of the undergraduate English major has after all been occurring in the context of a massive and malign rearrangement of the entire higher educational sector, from which heavily endowed private institutions like Yale are among the very few to enjoy any significant degree of insulation. In accordance with the global shift to a late-capitalist social and economic paradigm, academic labor (and particularly instructional labor) has been cheapened and casualized on a vast and international scale, while the fortunate few, atop the most elite enclaves, are enjoying unprecedented rates of compensation: a million dollars a year for university presidents, $3 million for superstar professors, and the sky's the limit for football coaches.[2] Students are lured to the most competitive private institutions with spacious campus apartments, organic cafeteria food, and state-of-the-art fitness centers, while their peers at under-resourced public institutions cannot even find seating space in the dilapidated lecture halls. For teachers and students alike, there has never been a wider gap between the haves and have-nots of the university system, nor so many who have next to nothing. If things look bad for English studies at Yale, what must they be like at Southern Connecticut State – or the University of Madras? And even these recent painful decades of productivity maximization and the market-driven, "customer service-oriented" retooling of academic programs have been in a sense a period of false hopes, transpiring within a millennial bubble of economic growth which has now been exposed as little more than a global Ponzi scheme. The bursting of this bubble in 2008, which exposed massive burdens of veiled debt, has brought new hardships to the educational sector and will likely lead to the closing of less advantaged departments and programs in the coming years, and even to the collapse of entire colleges and universities.

English literary study has certainly not been unscathed by this upheaval and transformation, and in some respects English clearly ranks among the system's zones of dispossession. Yet we should recognize that, in comparison with many disciplines, not just in the humanities but also in the social and natural sciences, English enjoys reasonably robust institutional health and fair prospects for the future. It holds some definite positional advantages which equip it to survive and even to advance its interests through the present turmoil.[3] Whether this is a happy state of affairs for higher education or for the world is a separate question, and one that deserves more serious and measured treatment than those of us who profess English for a living tend to give it. But to address that question honestly, we need a clearer view of our present circumstances and our actually possible trajectories. We need to move beyond our habitual posture of hand-wringing self-defense and self-justification toward genuine disciplinary reflexivity; beyond the normative thinking of a *discipline in crisis* toward a realistic appraisal of our choices and responsibilities as a *discipline with a future*.

No doubt that will be easier said than done. Our current anxieties are difficult to untangle from the deep, persistent, and perhaps even constitutive sense of institutional fragility and marginalization that has characterized English from the beginning. Ours is a discipline that has always believed to an extraordinary degree in its rightful centrality to the educational endeavor, and so has been forever struggling to account for and to overcome the perceived gap between its proper place and its actual institutional position. Practically since its first emergence as part of the higher educational curriculum, English studies has been issuing warnings and alarms regarding the grim realities of its current condition and the Herculean efforts that will be required to assure its survival and advancement. Already in the inaugural issue of *PMLA*, in 1884–1885, we find an example of what is now recognizable as one of the discipline's staple genres: the worried reckoning of a status deficit. Noting that "classics and mathematics retain for themselves the lion's share" of course requirements and student attention, the author, James M. Hart, sees English as relegated to a hopelessly minor place in the academic pecking order. This hierarchy, says Hart, is so entrenched institutionally that it is difficult to see any basis for raising "the hopes of our professors of literature," or to imagine any way that the position of English might be made

5

"capable of improvement" through internal reforms or classroom innovations. Unless the wrongful advantage enjoyed by rival disciplines is somehow lessened, the English curriculum "will remain perforce hurried and superficial," and it won't matter much how one adjusts the syllabus, the research methods, or the pedagogy.[4] More than a hundred years later, we find no less an authority on the discipline than Robert Scholes, himself soon to be president of the Modern Language Association (MLA), pronouncing English once again at a crisis point of low institutional status and collapsing intellectual legitimacy. "In the age of mass media," he observes, "literature has . . . lost its aura"; "English departments rode Pegasus to a position of academic prestige and relative affluence, but now, in our time, Pegasus has begun to look like other extremely large creatures with wings, that can run very fast but can't get off the ground. . . . We can either pretend, ostrichwise, that this hasn't happened or we can decide what to do about it."[5]

Scholes's broader analysis takes the form of a "rise-and-fall" narrative, treating the bulk of the years between Hart's gloomy diagnosis and his own as a period of conquest, marked by decisive institutional victories which saw our discipline seize the position of "academic prestige and relative affluence" that had formerly been enjoyed by classics. And indeed, the first six decades of the twentieth century witnessed, in Bill Readings's words, "the institutionalization of literature as bearer of the cultural task of the university," that is, the implementation of an educational ideology which figured literary study as the indispensable agent of both individual development and (national) social improvement.[6] But then, as this ideology gave way in the century's later decades to global neoliberal triumphalism, the value of "aesthetic education," both personal and social, began to lose its basis, its guarantee; the collective belief that had supported it was being withdrawn. English gradually ceded much of the ground it had won, not back to classics of course, but to new disciplines more closely aligned with professional training. Fields such as business management and the health sciences held out the promise of a more widely recognized and fungible form of value: increased "human capital" for the individual and hence greater "competitiveness" for the nation. English, meantime, no longer able to convincingly claim for itself the central and anchoring position among the disciplines, adopted a strategy of multiple positions, fostering a proliferation of new methods, materials, and constituencies, but, in the eyes of some, splintering itself across too broad an array of incompatible subfields, from book history to television studies, subcultural ethnography, and the poetics of race – squandering its disciplinary coherence and thereby further undermining its academic legitimacy.

This familiar narrative of the rise and fall of English is not mere fiction, but if it suggests an extended golden age during which collective anxieties about disciplinary legitimacy and long-term viability were held in abeyance, the archive tells us otherwise. As Gerald Graff described in his classic study of American English departments, *Professing Literature*, "A sense of crisis arose in the very midst of the heroic period of the literature department. . . . As early as the turn of the [twentieth] century, MLA addresses start to bewail the disappearance of the sense of solidarity and shared goals that had supposedly marked the first generation of modern language scholars of the [eighteen-]eighties and nineties."[7] And so it continued through the 1920s, 1930s, and 1940s, with each generation of English teachers and scholars perceiving a new crisis, or perceiving the same crises anew, of fragmented disciplinary identity, declining public legitimacy, and shaky institutional status. I will not rehearse that history here, but will point out that even the most recent crescendo of crisis narratives, which appeared in the wake of the culture and curriculum wars of the late 1980s and early 1990s (and which culminated with the substantial contributions of Readings and Scholes), itself coincided with a period of extraordinary growth and prosperity for English studies in the United States, when enrollments in the English major were rising faster than at any time in 30 years and faculty hiring, for a brief span, achieved near parity with the production of new PhDs. Where English is concerned, institutional success appears rather to stimulate than to dampen collective anxieties and grievances, exacerbating the sense that our place in the academy is fragile and threatened.

Which suggests, perhaps, that my own unwillingness to adopt the stance of crisis management here is driven by a kind of capitulative realism in the face of what is finally emerging as the moment of genuine meltdown, our last long slide into oblivion.[8] But despite all the challenges facing students and educators today, our discipline has not reached a precipice of especial vulnerability. If we step back from our local positions and consider the global future of English studies, there is little to suggest it is fading away. English is becoming an ever more dominant language of a rapidly expanding global higher education system. Anglophone literature is becoming an ever more integrated element of the global media system. New literatures in English are emerging, both inside and outside the horizon of metropolitan control. And the critical and methodological tools of English as a discipline are shaping much of the scholarly and pedagogical activity of emergent fields in the "post-disciplinary" humanities and social sciences. Though the specific position of English is subject to shifts on the wider academic landscape, the discipline appears, according to various reasonable metrics, to be firmly embedded in the terrain.

Nor, given the nature of these positional shifts and adjustments, will the survival of the discipline require the gutting of its foundational aims and values or the radical dismantling of its curriculum. The temporal slide of the syllabus toward more contemporary, more vernacular works will continue, to the disadvantage of certain "traditional" subfields. There will be constant internal conflict and struggle; as new pedagogical and research opportunities are recognized and seized, many current projects and tendencies will be shut down or abandoned. The expanding "basic" or "remedial" or "service" elements in the curriculum – freshman composition, business writing, English communication, English as a second language (ESL), and so on – will fight for status and autonomy, while the more "advanced" or "scholarly" or "high-cultural" elements attempt to guard their relative privilege. But what else is new? The forward creep of the syllabus, precisely at the expense of the "classics," is a tendency built into the very foundations of the discipline, as is the tension between the research-focused literature faculty and the rank-and-file writing instructors (even if the academy's increasingly ruthless exploitation of contingent labor means that this latter split can no longer be disguised in generational terms, as one between "masters" and "apprentices"). These internal struggles between contemporary and traditional material, between practical and intellectual "uses" of that material, between refinement of the literary habitus and attainment of basic, transportable skills, have helped to determine the very shape of our discipline and the course of its history. The fierce terms of intradisciplinary contention, no less than those of our new transdisciplinary articulations, can blind us to the enduring practices and problematics that constitute the disciplinary core of English studies, and that make it in many ways less fractured and less characterized by mutual incomprehension than other fields of higher education. The rhetoric of crisis tends to obscure the discipline's relative stability, leading us to imagine its unfolding future as a passage of pure rupture and transformation – or of tragic loss. The reality is that English has always been more substantially guided by inertia and ballast than we like to admit. It has contributed important innovations of method and has been a leading force for greater faculty diversity, but its institutional role is essentially that of a conservative rather than a transformative discipline. Certain basic academic dispositions, certain core beliefs (not excluding the belief in our "crisis"), and certain strong alliances on the field of power have persisted through decades of seeming tumult in English studies, and are not likely to erode any time soon.[9] Our future will be shaped as much by our discipline's conservatism as by its capacity for self-reinvention.

Let's Do the Numbers

If we are going to question the view of ourselves as standing on the brink of disciplinary collapse, we had better revisit the statistics that have been marshaled to support that view. Or, rather, it is a matter of looking carefully at numbers that have too often been ignored in favor of merely local or anecdotal forms of evidence. Deresiewicz's piece is typical in offering just a handful of frankly arbitrary and autobiographically oriented data points in support of the crisis hypothesis. It informs us that at one university, which happens to be the author's own, over one interval of time, which happens to coincide exactly with the author's period of employment there, enrollments in the English major fell from "about 120" per class cohort to "about ninety," and the number of faculty in English fell from "about fifty-five" to "about forty-five." Yale is certainly not a typical institution, and Deresiewicz offers no basis for generalizing from the experience at Yale to the national or global situation. No evidence is given to bolster the contentions that this 25% decline in majors and 18% drop in faculty (at one very atypical university) have been "prolonged," historically speaking, or that the declines are "irreversible," let alone that they are being driven by a sudden concern among students for "practical" skills which may be more readily acquired through "majors like economics." These kinds of statements cry out for some sort of statistical bolstering, but Deresiewicz knows that as an English professor he is not really expected to offer quantitative analysis. Ours is the great discipline of anecdote and conjecture. And since it is also the great discipline-in-crisis, the discipline that we all already believe to be in "steep decline," there is in this context even less call than usual for analytical rigor. One simply makes the jump, as Deresiewicz does, from a few recent and ultra-local observations to sweeping pronouncements on the fate of the discipline.[10]

This does not mean, however, that Deresiewicz is simply wrong about the enrollment crash in English since the mid-1990s. It would be surprising if the situation at Yale were a completely isolated case, and in fact it is not. The argument from local experience is persuasive because it chimes with many readers' experiences in their own institutional homes. But while Yale's numbers are in some ways representative, they can be profoundly misleading about the overall state of play in our discipline, not only because they happen to describe a sharper than normal decline but because the real trajectory of the field simply is not discernible from any of the specific institutional localities within it. Even if we could tally the sum experience of all the faculty in all the English departments everywhere over the past 10 years, we would still need to place those findings in the context of other disciplines' enrollments and hiring data in order to perceive our gains and losses in their properly relational terms. We would need as well to historicize recent tendencies in order to give statistical meaning to such terms as "steep" or "prolonged." And we would need to go beyond a merely national frame of analysis, since our discipline has long been and is becoming increasingly a global one in which both the "inputs" and "outputs" are international. North America and the United Kingdom offer wondrously abundant and robust higher educational data, and the states of those national fields of English studies have been well described over the years by government groups and professional association committees. But their relationship to each other, including some pronounced divergences and counter-tendencies, has generally not been addressed. Still less have these national cases been put into the context of English studies worldwide to consider whether the national trends are being amplified or offset by international developments, for example in such places as South and East Asia, where Anglophone higher educational programs have been rapidly expanding in recent years. Whatever future we aim to describe these days, whatever projection of rises and falls, or growth or shrinkage, in reference to higher education no less than to automobile production, we must take account of a global system.

The point of supplementing and contextualizing local field reports with large-scale data is not to abstract ourselves entirely away from the ground of local experience, where many of us really are facing urgent institutional problems. It is rather to arrive at an account of the discipline that clarifies the contours of that local ground and provides us with better tools for negotiating its pitfalls. Here is one quick example of what can be gained by a more statistical, less anecdotal perspective. Seeing a fall in English majors coinciding with a rise in economics majors at Yale, Deresiewicz concludes that students have been turning away from the former toward the latter. Others who have been seeing the same pattern at their universities in recent years – and it has been a fairly wide-spread one in the United States since the mid-1990s – might be inclined to accept this conclusion. The notion that prospective English majors have been fleeing to economics out of pragmatic capitulation to the triumph of free marketism is anecdotally persuasive.

But the numbers don't bear this out. Notwithstanding its trajectory of growth in recent years, economics has been struggling for much of the last quarter century with an enrollment crisis far more pronounced than our own. The problem has been severe enough to generate a substantial literature in the field, though in this case, as we would expect from economists, the crisis narratives have been less hectoring and prophetic and more textured by comparative statistical analysis.[11] One of the questions these researchers have attempted to address in quantitative terms is precisely that raised anecdotally by Deresiewicz, concerning interdisciplinary competition: against which other disciplines is economics most directly competing in the "curriculum marketplace"? By applying regression analysis to enrollment figures in nine major disciplines over a span of 28 years, they have found that the primary negative or "substitutive" correlate for economics, the discipline with which it is most directly "competing for students on the margin," is biology. English correlates most closely with history and psychology, but in a positive rather than a directly substitutive way. English and economics, meanwhile, do not correlate well at all; the choice between them is not one that students actually entertain to any statistically meaningful degree.[12]

This finding has a number of interesting implications, both analytical and strategic. Most obviously, it suggests that we should stop fretting about econ enrollments, which are an irrelevancy, and look to our relationship with history. The strongly positive correlations with history and with psychology mean that our enrollments can generally be expected to move up and down in tandem with theirs. In recent years, however, that has not been the case. Psychology, the largest of the three, has registered no

12

enrollment shift whatsoever, suggesting that this particular correlative cluster within the curricular marketplace is currently in a
steady state of demand and supply (when viewed as a percentage
share of total enrollments). But history enrollments have diverged
unexpectedly upward from this flat line, while English enrollments
have diverged unexpectedly downward.[13] One plausible interpreta-
tion of these data is that the pronounced historicist turn in English
studies, which began in the 1980s but required a decade or so of
generational turnover to become firmly lodged at the rank-and-file
level, has had the unintended effect of encouraging a mini-exodus
to history, where students perhaps can find a more evolved and
effective pedagogical model for the teaching of historical methods
and materials. Whatever its successes in scholarly or intellectual
terms, the prevailing historicism of the "post-formalist" and "post-
theory" period in English may be proving a failure in the
classroom. The current "crisis" may have less to do with a sudden
embrace of the practical or the lucrative on the part of our students
than with our own failures in making literature, as both a process
and an artifact of history, a sufficiently stimulating object for them
to study.[14] And this in turn suggests that the current (and still
rather inchoate) shift of the discipline away from historical and
political contextualism toward matters of form, reception, and
affect might eventually lead to a resurgence of undergraduate
enrollments.[15]

But we are getting ahead of ourselves, since the very shape and
extent of this putative crisis have yet to be determined. Let us
begin with student enrollments, a somewhat simpler matter than
faculty hiring. And for the moment let's focus on just the US
academy. The short answer to whether the decline at Yale is
indicative of a broad trend is no: nationwide, the number of graduating English majors actually rose by 12% between 1998 and 2008,
from about 49,000 to 55,000, and that increase came on top of
a more dramatic rise the decade before.[16] The longer answer is
much more complicated but enables us to say that yes, despite the
12% increase nationally, many English departments have seen their
majors shrink since the mid- to late 1990s. Even as we flesh out

that more nuanced and less encouraging view, however, we will find little justification for the rhetoric of crisis and collapse.

Thirty-five years ago, the enrollments data might well have supported such rhetoric, for we were indeed in the midst of a steep and decade-long decline. From a brief and heady high point in 1971, when there were 64,000 undergraduate degree takers in English, the numbers plummeted to 41,000 in 1976 and just 32,000 in 1981 – a drop of 50% from the all-time high. The discipline remained in this trough for a couple of years, but then began regaining most of the lost enrollments, climbing from 32,000 back to 51,000 between 1983 and 1991. Enrollments since then have held better than steady, trending slightly upward to hit the aforementioned figure of 55,000 in 2006, with little movement since then: a 72% rise from the 1981 bottom (see Figure 1.1).

Now of course, given the overall expansion of university enrollments during this entire period, a discipline that is simply maintaining its enrollments in absolute terms is experiencing declines in its relative share. The percentage of US university graduates who take their degrees in English, 3.5% in 2008, is less than half as large as it was in 1971, when it hit 7.6%. But given the host of new disciplines that have emerged and the much wider range of degree options that has become available to students, we would expect that latter figure to move downward over time. Nearly all the bread-and-butter liberal arts disciplines of the 1960s (including history, philosophy, political science, sociology, eco-nomics, math, biology, chemistry, and physics) have seen their slice of the enrollment pie significantly narrowed. Even with the new programs and departments that have emerged in the social sci-ences, the total share of graduates who take degrees categorized as "social sciences and history" has declined from 18.4% to just 10.5%. Math majors have dropped from 3% of graduates to less than 1%. The number of physics majors declined even in absolute terms through much of the 1980s and 1990s, hitting a 50-year low in 1999, and still lagging in relative terms despite gaining ground back since then.[17] Even economics, often wrongly invoked along-side business as one of the fast-rising disciplines, dropped from a

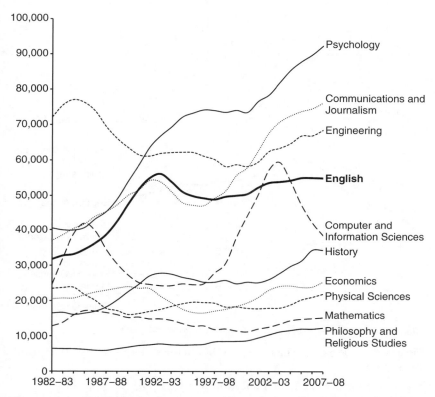

Figure 1.1 Bachelor's degrees conferred, by discipline, United States, 1983–2008.

Source: National Center for Education Statistics, *Digest of Education Statistics* 2009, Table 271.

2.1% share of graduates in 1970 to 1.6% in 1976, and hit its all-time low of 1.4% as recently as 1997. (See Figure 1.2; Figure 1.3 presents the number of majors together with the percentage share of majors on a single graph.)

These and similar declines in the liberal arts disciplines of the post-World War II academy have been driven mainly by gains in the health sciences (the popularity of which has also benefited the "soft science," psychology, especially during the rush toward health fields in the early to mid-1990s); in various new fields of

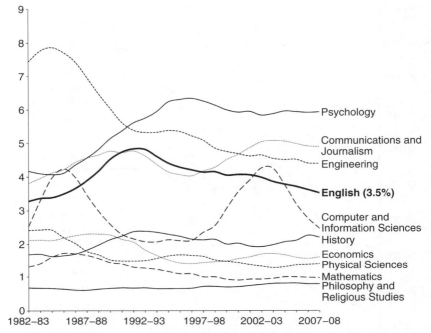

Figure 1.2   Percent share of US bachelor's degrees, by discipline, 1983–2008.

Source: National Center for Education Statistics, *Digest of Education Statistics* 2009, Table 271.

communications, media, and the visual and performing arts; and, above all, in the ever-widening range of essentially vocational programs in business and management, which now claim over 350,000 graduates a year, more than all the humanities combined. One could say that the proportional eclipse by such programs is indeed "irreversible"; we will never see 7.6% of college graduates taking their degrees in English again. On the other hand, once we accept this overall widening of the curricular spectrum and the formidable rise of business as achieved facts, we can observe that English has held its own, remaining one of the largest non-vocational degree programs as well as the largest by far in the humanities. Nor are the humanities eroding away, as many of us

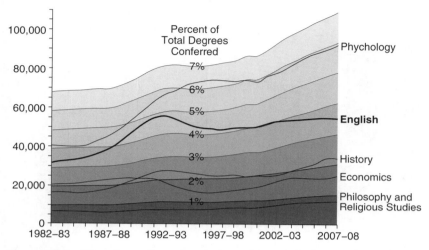

Figure 1.3 Number of graduating majors and share of total degrees, selected disciplines, United States, 1983–2008.
Source: National Center for Education Statistics, *Digest of Education Statistics* 2009, Table 271.

believe them to be. Support for a broad liberal arts education has been increasing across the entire academic profession, with community colleges in particular retooling their curricula away from narrow career training; the importance of teaching "moral values" as part of undergraduate education has likewise gained strength.[18] As a sector, the humanities has been the clear winner in the enrollments chase over the last 20–25 years, outperforming all the other sectors tracked by the National Center for Educational Statistics (NCES), including business.[19] (See Figure 1.4.) In short, considered strictly in terms of US higher educational enrollments over the past quarter century, English is the dominant field in the fastest rising sector, as well as a field whose share of undergraduate majors is larger than that of the combined computer and information sciences and larger than those of math, physics, chemistry, and geology put together.[20] This is not the scenario of a crisis.

Moreover, if we take a longer view of enrollment patterns, extending back to 1950, English appears remarkably stable. The

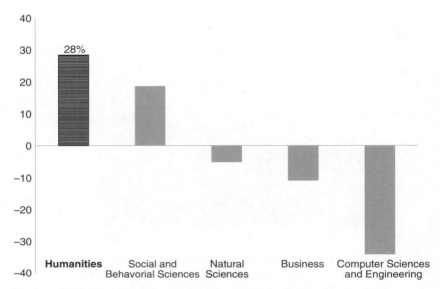

Figure 1.4 Percent change in share of undergraduate degrees granted, United States, 1983–2008.
Source: National Center for Education Statistics, *Digest of Education Statistics* 2009, Table 274.

discipline's share of total graduates in 1976, about 4.5 per 100, was virtually identical to its share 20 years earlier in 1956 as well as 20 years later in 1996. The fluctuations around this figure have been relatively modest, describing a range between the low-3% range and the high-4% range – with the one great exception of the sharp spike in the mid- to late-1960s, when enrollments doubled in the space of a few years. As the MLA's Ad Hoc Committee on the English Major argued in 2004, it has been an all too common mistake to treat this brief and plainly anomalous enrollment spike as the "standard against which subsequent developments should be measured."[21] What has occurred since then has not been the discipline's decline or slow death, but rather the expected return to a long-standing norm. Moreover, the causes of that releveling, as of the enrollment spike that preceded it, have less than is usually assumed to do with student attitudes toward the discipline of English. Enrollments rose dramatically in the 1960s when, for the first time, the university doors were fully opened to women students. That first generation of women for whom mass higher education was a reality still faced severe constraints on their career paths; they overwhelmingly chose majors linked to the traditional "caring" professions, in particular teaching. In 1966, women students were nearly three times as likely to major in English as men students (of whom only 4.4% chose English). Over the course of the next decade and a half, as the women's movement fought and won many hard battles over workplace access and equity, college-educated women increasingly entered the legal and medical professions as well as the management ranks of business and industry. Concomitant with these welcome developments was a diversification in women students' choices of majors. The percentage choosing English, though remaining somewhat higher than men's, fell dramatically toward the 4–5% range. The unusually large numbers of English majors during the spike years were mainly an effect of this (thankfully) short-term disconnect between women's educational opportunities and their professional ones.[22]

It is true that English has seen only modest enrollment increases since the early 1990s, when (buoyed in part by new requirements in some states that education students earn bachelor's degrees in the subject field they will be teaching) it briefly claimed more than 4.8% of all graduates.[23] While the discipline has continued to draw in more students, it has not kept pace with the growth of the educational system as a whole, which has increased its annual production of bachelor's degrees by 32% in the last decade, as compared to just 12% for English. (See Figure 1.5.) On the other hand, as already noted, if we open the time frame to 25 years instead of 10, we find English outpacing the overall growth rate, and expanding more rapidly than business, education, and most of the hard sciences. In fact, business, the monstrous predator of the education system, has increased its enrollments by only 43% since the mid-1980s, lagging behind the overall trajectory of expansion by nearly a third.[24] English meanwhile has expanded by almost

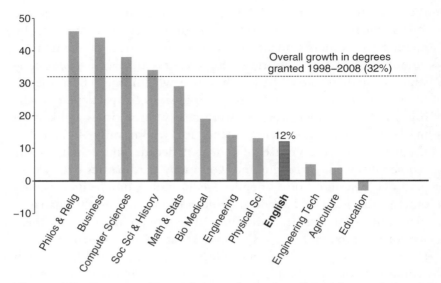

Figure 1.5   Percent change in number of undergraduate degrees granted, United States, 1998–2008.
Source: National Center for Education Statistics, *Digest of Education Statistics* 2009, Table 271.

70%, increasing its numbers about 15% faster than the system as a whole has done. (See Figure 1.6.)

We should note here, too, the important role of English in a number of emergent interdisciplinary fields. Though there are no nationwide statistics on the matter, it is clear that some significant fraction of the students who are pursuing their degrees in newer degree-granting fields such as cinema studies, ethnic studies, women's studies, cultural studies, African American studies, and Asian American studies are taking most of their classes in English and working predominantly with faculty in English. While they are not English majors, their intellectual formation is being guided more directly by English than by any other discipline, and to this extent they remain under the curricular umbrella of English studies. The numbers at issue are not large: about 7,500 students graduated from American universities with degrees in the relevant

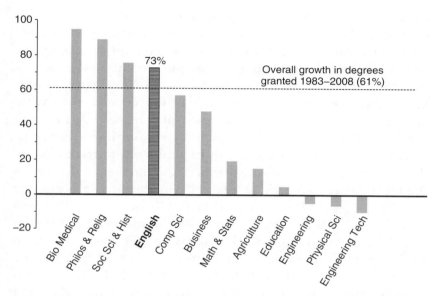

Figure 1.6 Percent change in number of undergraduate degrees granted, United States, 1983–2008.
Source: National Center for Education Statistics, *Digest of Education Statistics* 2009, Table 271; and *Digest of Education Statistics* 1995, Table 243.

subfields of "Area, Ethnic, Cultural, or Gender Studies" in 2008, and another 2,500 in the "Film/Cinema Studies" subfield within visual and performing arts. But these figures are rising rapidly, having increased more than 25% over the last decade.[25] They might be regarded as representing a small but nontrivial "hidden" fraction of English degree students.

How this situation looks and feels depends on where one stands. The overall growth of bachelor degree recipients from US colleges and universities – averaging 2.5% per year – has been very unevenly distributed. The rate of growth has been far more rapid among institutions of the Sunbelt than those of the Northeast or the Midwest, for example, and this is also where most of the new institutions and branch campuses have emerged. The private sector, though only about half the size of the public, has been growing

21

its enrollments more aggressively; but the lion's share of that growth has been in 4-year institutions other than research universities: liberal arts colleges, career schools, colleges of technology, and for-profit loan-scavenging pseudo-universities. At a private research university in the Northeast, such as Yale, where enrollments have been held steady for the last few decades, the overall growth of the system is a nonfactor, and relative declines are experienced as actual declines. At these universities (where the percentage of students majoring in English tends to track close to the national average), we could expect the number of degrees in English to have fallen by around 14% in the decade beginning in 1996; a department that graduated 120 majors in 1996 will likely have graduated about 103 in 2006. But that same department would have graduated only 94 students in 1986 (and only 90 in 1983), and remains within single digits of its 30-year average. Yale clearly experienced a sharper contraction than this, but then Yale is in many ways a special case. Owing to its illustrious tradition in the liberal arts, and in English specifically, it produces far more English majors than a typical Research I university (where the average is 4.5%). Its enrollment distribution more closely resembles that of a Liberal Arts I institution, where English typically claims twice as large a share of majors (9%) but has also been struggling to maintain that high level, and falling slowly back toward the national average in recent decades. These various trends can only partly explain a specific and local decline like Yale's.[26] But even at the "crisis" level of 2006, more than 7% of Yale's graduates were majoring in English. Long-overdue curricular reforms enacted in 2009 have already pulled up that figure significantly,[27] and the absolute numbers stand to rise a further 15% when Yale finally adjusts to the trend of expansion, as several of its immediate rivals have done, and opens two new residential colleges (scheduled for 2015). This is the kind of crisis a department can live with.

The recent decline in English's share of US bachelor's degrees is not good news, and bears watching closely over the next decade. But it is far from persuasive evidence in support of the "slow death" hypothesis. And outside the United States, such evidence is even scarcer. In fact, in a global frame, English appears to be a discipline on the rise. The United Kingdom, which as we would expect is the largest home to English majors in Europe, awarded 11,500 first degrees in English in 2009. This represents a 15% increase from 6 years earlier, and a steady share of all first degrees: 4.0%. The discipline is comfortably holding its own against the average. Looking at a somewhat longer time frame and at total enrollment figures rather than just degree takers, we find even more encouraging trends. According to annual data reported by the Higher Education Statistics Agency (HESA), enrollments in English more than doubled between 1998–99 and 2008–2009, from 25,888 full- and part-time English majors to 54,025.[28] This 109% increase is huge even in relative terms, since the overall rise in the number of undergraduate students during this period was only 29%, about the same as in the United States. (See Figure 1.7.)

Unfortunately, although HESA does distinguish between English and linguistics, it does not disaggregate English literature programs from English language (or combined English language and litera-ture) programs. It appears that some of the increased demand for English degrees is centered in English language studies,[29] which have gained from the rise of foreign students in UK universities (particularly in the years after 2001, when student visas to the United States became more difficult to obtain). This does not greatly distort the picture, however, since as I will discuss in Part III of the book, many English language programs also involve a considerable curricular component of English literary study. A more significant problem with the HESA statistics is that they began reflecting a new system for tabulating "combined" or joint majors in 2002–2003, now treating these students as enrollments in their primary field of study rather than segregating them in the "balanced combination" category that had been ballooning in size all through the 1990s. While this corrected a systemic undercounting of majors in English, history, and philosophy (the humanities subjects in which most of these students were actually concentrating their studies), it brought a sudden windfall on paper that reflects no actual change in the classrooms.[30] HESA never

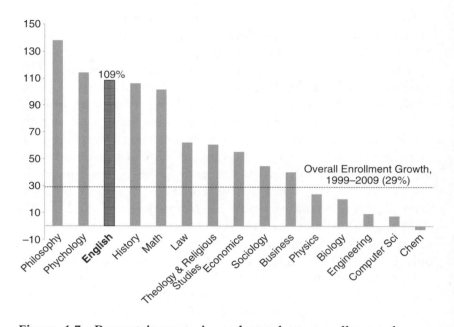

Figure 1.7 Percent increase in undergraduate enrollments by discipline, United Kingdom, 1999–2009 – unadjusted HESA statistics.

Source: Higher Education Statistics Agency, various tables.

attempted to adjust their earlier numbers to correct for these undercounts, but we can project the current counting system backward from 2002 and arrive at reasonable estimates for English (which, as counted by the new method, would have had about 12,000 more students in 1998–1999) and for all other affected disciplines. After making these recalculations, we still find English among the fastest growing disciplines, outpacing the overall rate of growth in higher education by a large margin. Though psychology has been the standout growth major in the United Kingdom (as it was somewhat earlier in the United States), English has expanded more rapidly than history, business, or economics, and much more rapidly than sociology, most of the physical sciences, computer science, or engineering. (See Figure 1.8.)[31]

24

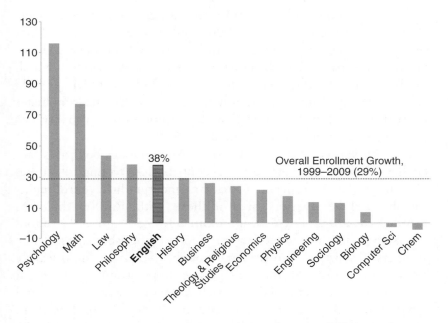

Figure 1.8 Percent increase in undergraduate enrollments by discipline, United Kingdom, 1999–2009 – adjusted HESA statistics.

Source: Higher Education Statistics Agency, various tables.

Looking at broader trends in Britain, there is no evidence for a flight from English or from other humanistic fields to more "practical" ones. On the contrary, HESA's former "Humanities" category (now labeled "Historical and Philosophical Studies"), which includes various programs of historical study, including history of art and history of science, as well as philosophy and archeology, has experienced undergraduate enrollment growth of nearly 70%, from 47,000 in 1997 to 80,000 in 2008, with philosophy gaining share even faster than English has done, from 4,100 to 9,400 or an increase of 125%.[32] Overall, language and literature programs, of which English studies is by far the largest, have grown by 50%, and even with English removed from the mix they have kept pace with the overall expansion.

25

These are undergraduate enrollment figures rather than numbers of first degrees granted; at 12,000 English degree recipients per year, the UK graduates barely a fifth of the US number. Despite the recent expansion of Britain's higher education system, which has brought it to the point where 43% of adults under 30 hold degree-level qualifications, the system's 2 million undergraduates are still dwarfed by the more than 18 million enrolled in degree-granting institutions in the United States.[33]

The university systems of other Anglophone countries are smaller still, making their statistical contributions to English studies accordingly less significant. Canadian undergraduate enrollments are about three quarters of a million, with 161,000 diplomas awarded in 2007, of which approximately 5,500 (or 3.4%, about the same as in the United States) went to English majors.[34] The numbers in Australia are similar (though involving a significantly higher proportion of the college-age population), with about 600,000 students enrolled in bachelor's degree programs and 155,000 bachelor's degrees awarded in 2009.[35] 17,000 of these students were majoring in "Language and Literature," with the bulk of those in 3-year English BA programs. Without access to disaggregated graduation data, we can only make a very rough estimate that 4,000 of the bachelor's degrees awarded in 2009, or about 2.6%, went to students majoring in English. English enrollments appear to be keeping pace with overall enrollment growth and the broader disciplinary category under which literature majors are classified, "Society and Culture" is the largest after "Management and Commerce" and has been increasing at about the same rate as total bachelor's enrollments. Language and Literature majors rose about 9% between 2004 and 2009, versus 7% growth of overall domestic enrollments and 12.5% of overall enrollments if the international students (mostly East Asians doing degrees in business) are included. The broader disciplinary category under which literature majors are classified, "Society and Culture," has been booming for the last decade.[36]

Combined English enrollments of the United States, United Kingdom, Canada, and Australia currently produce about 75,000

BA graduates per year and climbing. These are the traditional, more or less stable national homes of English studies, and the bases of its most prestigious and well-funded departments in the Anglophone world. Even across these relatively homogeneous departments there is considerable variety, but taken together they house the form of English studies that most closely approximates to our traditional idea of the discipline.

This does not mean, however, that the discipline dissolves or is transformed into something altogether different at these country's borders. English is a well-established and popular discipline in many countries where it is predominantly taught as a foreign language – especially in Western Europe and in some of the former British colonies – and these, too, must be considered among its traditional homes. While the number of students pursuing English degrees has been increasing in what we might call its "domestic base," its more dramatic and sustainable growth is to be located in these established foreign locations, together with a number of newly emergent ones. Among other important factors, English serves in these countries as a leading discipline for future primary and secondary school teachers. And not only is the demand for teachers increasing in the dozens of countries with growing populations and/or gaps to close between current enrollment rates and the goal of Universal Primary Education (UPE), but the demand for teachers with proficiency and expertise in English is especially acute and rising rapidly nearly everywhere with the spread of English as a global lingua franca.[37] These non-Anglophone countries are the sites through which the trajectory of English studies must be projected; they will have a large role to play in determining its future forms and functions.

Not a Bust but a Boom

Our brief statistical survey of English enrollments must therefore extend beyond what has generally been the comfort zone for the discipline's commentators and historians. We can begin with continental Europe, where higher educational enrollments have been rising much more rapidly than in the United States, and where many thousands of 3.5- or 4-year degrees in English are conferred each year.[38] It could be argued that English studies has its origins as a university discipline in Europe no less than in Great Britain and its colonies. (The same may be said of American literary and cultural studies, which dates back more than a century in France, gained much of its contemporary curricular status under the impetus of the United States' Cold War cultural initiatives in Western Europe during the 1950s, gained popularity among students and professors of English throughout Europe during the 1960s, and is today a major subfield if not a core requirement of most European programs in English studies.)[39] To be sure, and as will be detailed in Part III of this book, English as a foreign language discipline differs from domestic English studies in its curricular content and structure, as well as in its relationships to other disciplines. But as the editors of the *European Journal of English Studies* recently remarked, while "it can be misleading in a number of ways to consider 'English' as exactly the same discipline in the UK, in Ireland, and in non-Anglophone Europe . . . it cannot be considered in each case a discipline apart from that practiced in the others."[40] The discipline consists in the entire system or network of articulations across the many lines of national difference.

A majority of the bachelor's or BA-equivalent programs in continental Europe offer English as a combined degree option, or a specialist option within various other major disciplines; only a fraction of students studying English in European universities take free-standing bachelor's degrees in English.[41] Still, the latter numbers are by no means negligible and they appear to be rising. In France, for example, statistics reported by the National Education Ministry in the mid-1990s indicate about 600,000 students specializing in English within other major degree programs and 50,000 pursuing 3-year or higher degrees in English studies itself. There were annually 6,600 students of English sitting the CAPES exam (for certification as secondary school teachers), 1,300 sitting the far more competitive and prestigious *Agrégation*, and 130 completing doctoral dissertations.[42] These numbers are not much smaller than those of Great Britain back in the mid-1990s, and the years since then have seen steadily rising higher education enrollments in France, from about 1.6 million in 1991 to 2 million in 2001 and 2.2 million in 2008 – suggesting current cohorts in English studies may be 20% or 30% larger than in the 1990s. "By any measure," comments Imelda Bonel-Elliott in her 2000 survey, "English studies represent a vast enterprise in France."[43]

Other European countries are running more modest operations in English than this, but their overall enrollments have in many cases been rising much faster. In Greece, for example, the percentage of 18 to 21 year olds pursuing bachelor's degrees more than doubled in the space of a decade, 1993–2004.[44] English studies has a firm institutional position in Germany, which possesses the region's second-largest higher educational system after France, and it is a significant curricular presence in Spain, Greece, Italy, the Netherlands, Sweden, Finland, and other countries of Northern Europe. English has been a fast-rising discipline in post-Soviet Central and Eastern Europe as well, particularly in the large Polish university system, which graduates a higher percentage of its college-aged population than the United States or the United Kingdom, and confers nearly as many degrees as France. While no country in Europe grants as high a proportion of its bachelor's degrees to English majors as the Anglophone nations do, the European tertiary system as a whole is larger and faster growing than the combined systems of North America, Australia, and the United Kingdom, and it accounts for several tens of thousands of English degree recipients every year.

Traditionally, these European graduates, together with those from the Anglophone countries, constituted nearly the entire world cohort of annual degree takers in English studies. But as both the number of English speakers and the scale of higher educational apparatus increase outside this traditional disciplinary base, substantial new or greatly expanded sites of English studies are opening up. Worldwide, enrollments in tertiary education have exploded since the 1980s, surpassing even the formidable increases of Europe.

Many countries in Asia and the Global South have seen significant population growth in the 19–25 age cohort, but those demographics have played much less of a role in driving the enrollment boom than global pressure toward higher "gross enrollment rates" (GERs): rates of participation as a percentage of the college-age population. A high GER, of at least 40–50% and preferably much higher, has come to be embraced by UNESCO, the World Bank, the World Trade Organization, and other international institutions as a key to economic growth and development. In countries where secondary education has become effectively universal, and especially in those where middle-class populations have been rising, this macro pressure on developing nations is strongly reinforced by internal popular demand as more and more families come to view access to higher education as a necessity for their children. Just as occurred with primary and later with secondary education, tertiary education has been reframed, in global terms, as a basic right or entitlement.

Even in countries like Finland and the United States, which have long had GERs above 60%, there has still been room for expansion of this kind (and, indeed, some countries' GERs could eventually rise above 100% since the ratio includes "nontraditional" students who enter the system from outside the specified age range). But many countries, starting from much lower ratios (some in the single digits), have more than tripled their GERs over the past 2–3 decades; a few, such as South Korea, have leapt from single digits to nearly 100% gross enrollment in the space of a single generation.[45] As a result of this broad trend toward massification, total tertiary enrollments worldwide increased from about 50 million at the start of the 1980s to nearly 150 million in 2007, climbing 43% in North America, 100% in Europe, nearly 300% in Central and South America, 400% in Asia, and 500% in Africa.[46] (See Figure 1.9.) We need to look to these areas, and especially to South and East Asia (where the absolute numbers are largest), if we are to have any real sense of what future enrollments in English are likely to be.

I will here consider just the two largest countries, India and China, which together account for nearly a third of the world's

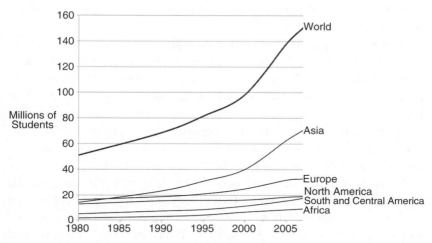

Figure 1.9   Total tertiary enrollments, 1980–2007, worldwide and by region.

Source: National Center for Education Statistics, *Digest of Education Statistics* 2009, Table 397; adapted by NCES from UNESCO, *Statistical Yearbook*, 1999; and unpublished tabulations.

tertiary enrollments outside the United States and Europe. It is now well known that India served as the original colonial laboratory for the incubation of English studies nearly two centuries ago. As Gauri Viswanathan has described, the Indian university system evolved from a trickle-down or "filtration" theory of culture that staked the whole colonial enterprise on the creation of a morally elevated tier of Indians "trained to a high level of excellence in the study of English literature."[47] But almost from the start, and well into the twentieth century, this project was riven by serious doubts as to the efficacy of such a system, which appeared to produce an elite Anglophone class that was disdainful of the vernacular and largely insulated from the concerns of the masses, possessed of aesthetic refinements which ill equipped them for the practical tasks of governance and industry: an indirect ruling class whose ostensive "moral education" rendered them incapable of serving either as disseminators of Western culture (seed figures

31

of a general enlightenment) or as competent leaders of a modern political and economic order.

In part because of its central if controversial role in the university system during the period of its colonial gestation, English studies found its place in that system even more strenuously contested in the postcolonial era, when the hegemony of the English language in global intellectual exchange was regarded as a key weapon in the arsenal of neo-imperial domination and English studies as the curricular linchpin of the Anglophone academic order. But with the waning of the postcolonialist paradigm in India as elsewhere, there has occurred a shift whereby the English language is seen to represent India's expanding place in the traffic of the world rather than its enduring subjugation to British norms, values, and hierarchies. As Kailash Baral puts it, "English has moved from being the subject of politics to an object of economic empowerment."

> Globalization has brought in its wake a radical change in the attitudes of people toward English in all walks of life, including those who were earlier opposed to it. Instead of being a symbol of imperialism and identified with a certain class or caste of people, English is now considered as the language of opportunity, thanks to multinational corporations, free trade, and outsourcing of software services. It is one of the most sought after curricular subjects as each state in the country, in spite of the ideological inclinations of the ruling class, has started acknowledging its functional primacy.[48]

While, as Braj Kachru has observed, there remains in India as elsewhere in the Global South "a lingering Trojan-horse association with the language and its managers," English has become so incontestably the "access" language of our economic world system that the linguistic question is no longer whether but how to appropriate or deploy it outside the metropole.[49] In India, this easing of the tensions and anxieties around English as the official language of higher learning has coincided with a dramatic (though badly mismanaged and under-funded) expansion of the country's post-

32

secondary educational system. Even a very conservative estimate puts the number of full-time undergraduates enrolled in that system at 10 million, with close to 2 million students taking college degrees in 2006.[50] The quality of these degrees has been called into doubt even within India. The educational system has been severely strained by its rapid expansion, and the government has failed to meet the challenges of massification in terms of either funding or leadership. Into this vacuum have rushed many incompetent or unscrupulous entrepreneurs, who have met the rising demand for higher education with ad hoc private institutions which, though often linked to state universities, are geared entirely toward profit. These "affiliated colleges" now number in the tens of thousands and operate for the most part beyond the reach of any supervisory or regulatory system.[51] In many ways, some of which will be discussed in Part II of the book, India stands as a warning or a negative lesson rather than a positive example for global academe and for global English studies in particular. Nevertheless, with respect to our narrow concern here – the trajectory of enrollments – the country is a huge engine of growth. In engineering and science, it has emerged as a clear world leader, producing more engineering graduates than the United States not only in absolute terms but also (astonishingly) even when measured per capita. Its English majors do not by any means represent as large or institutionally well supported a fraction, comprising no more than a small percentage of total enrollments. Data are scarce, but even 2% of 2 million, a reasonable estimate, would be 40,000 English graduates a year. That's four times as many as in the United Kingdom, and at current rates of growth will surpass the United States by 2012. There is no reason to expect these growth rates to slacken, either, given that the level of participation in India's tertiary education system, currently approaching a 2012 goal of 12% of the relevant age population, is barely a quarter of the GER target recommended by the World Bank, and an even farther cry from the rates of the wealthiest nations.[52] And the kind of external pressure that comes from organizations like UNESCO and the World Bank, who caution that India's world-beating

33

economic ambitions cannot be achieved without the development of a world-class higher education system, is nothing compared to the internal pressures for greater access, which are intensifying in India as elsewhere. Recent government committee reports propose "a goal of doubling the higher educational capacity from the present level."[53] Despite the phenomenal rate of recent expansion, this is a country whose academic apparatus is still at a relatively early point on the growth curve.

China has been expanding its higher education system even faster, bringing its tertiary enrollment ratio up from 3% of the age cohort in 1991 to nearly 20% in 2005 — more than three times the rate of increase in India.[54] And, since the turn of the twenty-first century, China has been investing far more public money than India on new faculty and new infrastructure, and has been setting ambitious targets for improving quality as well as expanding access.[55] It remains to be seen whether reasonable quality standards can be achieved in the face of such rapid growth, particularly among the many local and especially private colleges that have absorbed much of the enrollment increases. But there is little doubt that China's major public research universities are improving. Unlike most other developing nations (including India), China has hinged its economic development strategy less on primary and secondary than on tertiary education, and even on the most advanced end of the tertiary spectrum.[56] But whatever its internal stratifications, the sheer scale of the system makes it vital to the future of global academe. The county already has more post-secondary students enrolled than any other — somewhere around 25 or 30 million, up from just 1 million in 1998 and 19 million in 2004.[57] Whereas the American universities graduated fewer than 2 million students with baccalaureate degrees in 2008, China graduated more than 3 million.

Within this huge system, English is a durable and popular subject, having survived the evisceration of the universities during the period of the Cultural Revolution (which began in 1966, just when the English major enjoyed its great surge of popularity in the United States and other Anglophone countries) to become the single largest motor of growth for global English studies. In the early 1980s, there were fewer than 20,000 English majors in China. By 1996, that number had topped 50,000, and today it is estimated to be over 500,000, more than twice as many as in the United States and about 10 times as many as in the United Kingdom.[58] The number of students in English bachelor's degree programs has been rising even faster than the number of institutions offering such programs (up from 304 English BA programs in 1999 to 420 in 2002 and roughly 1000 in 2010), and, given China's ambitious spending plans and growth targets, is likely to rise a bit further in the next decade, despite the now shrinking population of 15 to 19 year olds and the dimmer employment prospects for graduates holding degrees in English.[59]

Even within Asia, we could greatly elaborate this picture of future enrollments in English studies. I have yet to mention Hong Kong, Taiwan, Singapore, or Korea, each of which has a highly developed curriculum in English studies and a distinct situation with respect to current and future enrollment ratios. And then we have not considered Mexico or South America, home to some 13 million undergraduates and hundreds of English departments, or the small but fast-growing university systems in African countries like South Africa, Nigeria, and Kenya, where English claims an even larger share of majors than it does in the United States or the United Kingdom. Some of these places will be discussed in Part III, which treats the varied curricular options and emphases that share space under the rubric of English studies. But the point I hope to have made clear enough already, as summarized in Figures 1.10 and 1.11, is that, in absolute terms, English is a growing rather than a shrinking discipline, and especially so when considered in a global perspective. It is an integral part of an ongoing and unprecedented boom in the world's tertiary educational system. The challenges it faces are not at all those of decline or "slow death," but rather those associated with the global mandate for radically expanded access: the challenges of declining selectivity of admissions, intensifying curricular stress on basic and remedial education, widening disparity between upper and lower

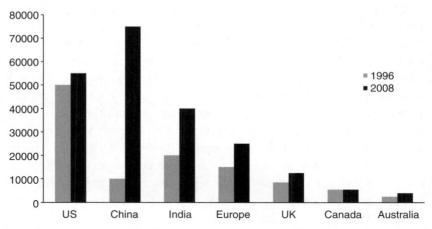

Figure 1.10   Number of graduating English majors in selected countries and regions, 1996 and 2008.

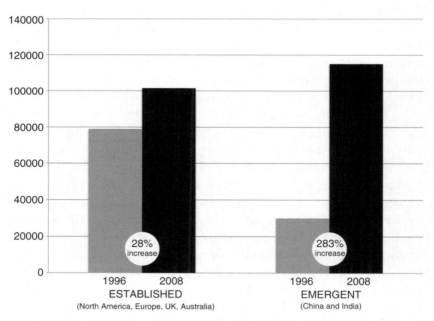

Figure 1.11   Number of graduating English majors, 1996 and 2008, by broad groups of countries.

academic echelons, and a rising ratio of students to instructional dollars.

Notes

1. William Deresiewicz, "Professing Literature in 2008," *The Nation*, 11 March 2008.

2. According to various online lists, including those on *America's Best & Top Ten*, Mack Brown, head coach of the University of Texas football team, earned $5.1 million in 2010. There are more than 30 football and basketball coaches earning $2 million or more, and many assistant coaches earn over $1 million. Similar compensation goes to the investment officers who manage university endowments; the top two investment officers at Yale earned a combined $10 million in 2009. Among university presidents, *Business Week* reports that Vanderbilt's E. Gordon Gee earned $2.1 million in 2006–2007, but took a pay cut when he left for Ohio State, where his 2009–2010 compensation was $1.58 million. As for faculty, leading professors in medicine and the health sciences earn even more than presidents, with some, such as Zev Rosenwaks of Cornell, topping $3 million. Even in the humanities and social sciences, there are faculty earning half a million dollars, for example economics professors David Levine and Michele Boldrin at Washington University. High-end salaries are less extreme outside the United States, but top business faculty in Canada can earn more than $300,000, and in Singapore more than $200,000. See Jeffrey Brainard, "Biggest Campus Paycheck May Not Be the President's," *Chronicle of Higher Education* 55 (20 February 2009): A1; Tamar Lewin, "Many Specialists at Private Universities Earn More than Presidents," *New York Times* 22 February 2009; and Gregory Clark, "Dismal Scientists: How the Crash Is Reshaping Economics," *The Atlantic*, online edition, 16 February 2009.

3. As American universities continue to adjust to the bleak economic landscape not just with across-the-board budgetary belt tightening but also by making "vertical cuts" that eliminate entire programs and departments, a kind of endangered disciplinary species list is emerging. English does not appear on this list, and simply is not vulnerable in the way that departments of German, philosophy,

political science, and sociology (among others) appear to be. See Robin Wilson, "In Hard Times, Colleges Search for Ways to Trim the Faculty: Why Certain Departments Fall under the Budget Ax," *Chronicle of Higher Education* 26 June 2009.

4. James M. Hart, "The College Course in English Literature: How It May Be Improved," *PMLA* 1 (1884–1885): 84–95. I first came across this piece in Rita Raley's online "History of English Studies Page," still a useful resource though no longer up to date. The page may be accessed at http://www.english.ucsb.edu/faculty/ rraley/research/englstud.html.

5. Robert Scholes, *The Rise and Fall of English* (New Haven: Yale University Press, 1998), 164.

6. Bill Readings, *The University in Ruins* (Cambridge, MA: Harvard University Press, 1996), 73

7. Gerald Graff, *Professing Literature: An Institutional History* (Chicago: University of Chicago Press, 1987), 99, 110.

8. As argued most passionately by Frank Donahue, *The Last Professors: The Corporate University and the Fate of the Humanities* (New York: Fordham University Press, 2008). Donahue eschews the term "crisis" as too "dramaturgic," pointing out that the corporatization of American academe has been an "ongoing process" for more than a century. Nevertheless, his self-described "sepulchral" analysis foresees a day in the not-too-distant future when English as a field of research and an option for the professorial career has disappeared altogether from the American higher educational landscape. For another example of the genre, see William M. Chace, "The Decline of the English Department," *The American Scholar* 1 September 2009. Chace, a former president of Wesleyan and Emory, follows the usual procedure of treating the aberrant spike of the late 1960s and early 1970s as the basis from which all statistical "facts" about English enrollments must be derived.

9. This book can be seen as an attempt to elaborate in a different and more empirical way an argument about the history of the discipline that I first made a few years ago: that for all its internal struggles and disputes, literary studies has been shaped by a powerful conservatism as to its central commitments and claims, a conservatism that is by no means limited to right-wing or rear-guard factions, and that has undoubtedly helped to stabilize the discipline's institutional position through a period of rapid change. James F.

English, "Literary Studies," in Tony Bennett and John Frow, eds., *Handbook of Cultural Analysis* (London: Sage, 2008), 126–144.

10. Another instance of the crisis narrative flying in the face of statistical reality was an address on the "disappearance of the English department," given by the chair of the Conference on College Composition and Communication (CCCC) at the CCCC annual convention in 2004. In "Made of More than Words," Kathleen Yancey raised an alarm saying that since the mid-1980s there had been "a decline in the number of departments called English of about 30%." As our discipline's most authoritative statistician, David Laurence, carefully elaborated in "The Evidence Is Not There," *College Composition and Communication* 57.2 (2005): 358–360, this was "a statement that has no citation or documentation and that information from available sources . . . shows to be seriously in error" (360).

11. Much of the scholarship addressing economics enrollments focuses on the period from the late 1980s to the mid-1990s, which saw the discipline's share of degrees fall from 2.3% to 1.4%, an all-time low. See John J. Siegfried, "Trends in Undergraduate Economics Degrees, 1991 to 2003," *Journal of Economic Education* 35 (2004): 304–308.

12. Hirschel Kasper, "Sources of Economics Majors: Less Business, More Biology," *Southern Economic Journal* 75 (2008): 457–472, especially Table 1 and discussion on 462. Kasper cautions that his conclusions regarding biology's substitutive relationship to economics are merely provisional.

13. I am speaking here of percentage share rather than absolute numbers of students. Between 2001 and 2008, all three disciplines saw their enrollments climb with the overall expansion of the American higher educational system. In the case of psychology, the increase was exactly proportionate with the system as a whole: the discipline's share of degrees conferred, 5.9% in 2001, remained 5.9% in 2008. History's share rose from 2.0% to 2.25%, while English's share fell from 4.0% to 3.5%. It seems reasonable to speculate that about half of the .5% decline of English's share of graduates has migrated to the history major.

14. On the virtues of formalism and close reading for purposes of undergraduate teaching, see Jane Gallop, "The Historicization of Literary Studies and the Fate of Close Reading," *Profession*

(2007): 181–186. Aside from noting our relative lack of skill at teaching history (183), Gallop argues that a pedagogy centered on close reading is less dependent on students' previous training and cultural literacy; the New Criticism was in this sense "a great leveler of cultural capital."

15. This turn from the project of sociohistorical contextualization toward matters of form, affect, and the experience of reading can be seen in an earlier Blackwell Manifesto, Rita Felski's *Uses of Literature* (Oxford: Blackwell, 2008).

16. US Department of Education, National Center for Education Statistics (NCES), *Digest of Education Statistics* (Washington, DC: NCES, 2009), Table 271: "Bachelor's Degrees Conferred by Degree-Granting Institutions, by Field of Study: Selected Years, 1970–71 through 2007–08." Figures 1.1, 1.2, and 1.3 are based on the corresponding table, Table 282, from the 2010 *Digest*. Subsequent citations to the *Digest*, an annually updated and archived online resource (http://nces.ed.gov/programs/digest/), will be given as NCES, *Digest of Education Statistics*, with year.

17. Both the American Institute of Physics' Statistics Resource Center (http://www.aip.org/statistics) and the National Center for Educational Statistics put the discipline's all-time low point at 1998–1999, with a recovery since then back to mid-1980s levels (but still below the early-1970s numbers, even in absolute terms). Domestic enrollments are so low at the undergraduate level that more than half of the students in US doctoral programs are recruited from foreign bachelor's programs. For a quick overview of the problems facing physics as a discipline, with particular emphasis on the poor pedagogical practices in physics departments at research universities, see Jack M. Wilson, "The Physics Major: An Endangered Species?" *Forum on Education Newsletter* (American Physical Society) (Spring 2002): http://www.aps.org/units/fed/newsletters/spring2002/wilson.html.

18. Martin J. Finkelstein and Jack H. Schuster, *The American Faculty* (Baltimore: Johns Hopkins University Press, 2006), 131–132.

19. Figure 1.4 is based on NCES, *Digest of Education Statistics* 2009, Table 274: "Bachelor's, Master's, and Doctor's Degrees Conferred by Degree-Granting Institutions, by Field of Study and Year: Selected Years, 1970–71 through 2007–08." Looking at the corresponding table in the more recently released 2010 *Digest* (Table

285), we can see that since 1986, the humanities have increased their share of all bachelor's degrees by nearly a third, from 13.5% to 17.5%; the social and behavioral sciences have seen a more moderate increase from 13.6% to 16.4%; the natural sciences have been unchanged; and education, business, and "computer sciences and engineering" have all experienced significant declines. Unlike the social and behavioral sciences, the humanities have continued to grow all through the 1990s and into the new century, this growth driven in large part by the expansion of programs in the subcategory of "visual and performing arts."

20. The narratives of crisis in the humanities often seem to imply that the US education system has become excessively tilted in the direction of science and technology. Just the opposite is the case. "Tertiary Graduates in Science and Technology per 1000 Persons aged 20-29," a key figure in international comparisons, is notably low in the United States, about half the rate of the United Kingdom and France, and, according to the most recent data from Eurostat (http://epp.eurostat.ec.europa.eu), it has been falling since 2003.

21. ADE Ad Hoc Committee on the English Major, "The Undergraduate English Major," *Profession 2004* (2004): 178–217, quote from 211.

22. For the statistics, see MLA, *Report to the Teagle Foundation on the Undergraduate Major in Language and Literature*, February 2009, 20, Figure 5, http://www.mla.org/pdf/2008_mla_whitepaper.pdf.

23. I have not found good national data on English education enroll-ments, but the ADE's Ad Hoc Committee report, "The Undergraduate English Major," hazards a "hypothesis [that] the increases and declines in English baccalaureate degrees between 1987 and 1997 are connected to the numbers of baccalaureate degrees in education, and the waxing and waning of student inter-est in secondary school teaching" (188).

24. Nor have the large master's programs in business provided a reliable counterweight to this trend. The *Chronicle of Higher Education* reported in its September 2, 2005, issue that, after peaking in 2002, applications to full-time MBA programs had fallen steadily, and that the number of students taking the GMAT exam had fallen nearly 25%. A 2005 survey by *Business Week* found that among leading MBA programs, enrollments had fallen an average of 30%

since 2001. See Tracy Carbasho, "After Years of Decline, MBA Enrollment Figures Could Rise Again," *Pittsburgh Business Times*, 27 May 2005.

25. These are rough estimates based on numbers in the NCES *Digest of Education Statistics* 2010. For the broad growth trend, see Table 282: "Bachelor's Degrees Conferred by Degree-Granting Institutions, by Field of Study: Selected Years, 1970–71 through 2008–09"; for the breakdown into individual subfields, see Table 286: "Bachelor's, Master's, and Doctor's Degrees Conferred by Sex of Student and Discipline Division, 2008–09."

26. National figures are taken from the ADE report, "The Undergraduate English Major." The sharper than expected decline at Yale has been attributed to the department's anachronistic curriculum, which, prior to a substantial overhaul in 2009, overemphasized English poetry and literature before 1800, and failed to meet strong student demand for courses in post-1900 fiction. On this, see Yale College, "January 2008: Report on the English Major," http://yalecollege.yale.edu/content/january-2008-report-english-major.

27. According to the department's chair, Michael Warner, in a June 2011 email, there has been a "definite uptick" since the reforms, with enrollments "rising at about the rate [they] used to decline."

28. Higher Education Statistics Agency (HESA), *Students in Higher Education Institutions 1998/1999*, Table 2e: "All HE Students by Subject of Study, Domicile, and Gender 2008/2009"; and HESA, *Students in Higher Education Institutions 1999/2000*, Table 2e: "All HE Students by Subject of Study, Domicile, and Gender 2008/2009." Both are available online from the HESA Publications Archive at http://www.hesa.ac.uk/index.php?option=com_content&task=view&id=801&Itemid=250. Subsequent references to HESA's annually updated and archived statistical tables will use the abbreviation "HESA" with dates and table numbers.

29. Judith Baxter and Denise Santos, "English Language at Undergraduate Level: Its Identity as a Subject in UK Higher Education in the 21st Century," research report of the Subject Centre for Languages, Linguistics, and Area Studies, Higher Education Academy (York, UK: Higher Education Academy, 2008), http://www.llas.ac.uk/projects/2948. The Quality Assurance Agency (QAA) for Higher Education is currently working on a

better way to classify programs in and around English, but it is unlikely that whatever new system emerges can be projected backward to produce a clear sense of historical enrollment trends within the discipline's various subdivisions.

30. There was, however, a very widespread actual expansion in those years. A snapshot of UK English departments in 2003 indicates that most departments anticipated increased enrollments for the coming year and nearly two thirds had experienced rising enrollments over the previous 5 years. A further finding of this survey is that three quarters of all English departments were "net gainers" in respect of transfers from one discipline to another within their institution, while only 4% were net losers. One might tentatively infer that English stands to gain from the global trend toward increasing student and consumer "choice," as students are permitted more latitude to select their major *after* arriving at university. And this trend will be strongly reinforced in Britain with implementation of the new policies laid out in the Browne Report. See Halcrow Group, Ltd., *Survey of the English Curriculum and Teaching in UK Higher Education*, LTSN English Subject Centre Report Series 8, October (Egham, UK: LTSN English Subject Centre, 2003), 11, Table 2.10, and 12, Table 2.12.

31. In the first year of the new counting system (2002–2003), reported English enrollments, full-time plus part-time, jumped from about 30,000 to 48,000, and certain other disciplines were also dramatically affected (HESA Table 2e, 2002/2003). To correct for this distortion, I assumed that the actual increases and declines for that year were about the same (in percentage terms) as the average of the year just before and the year just after. I then worked backward from the 2002–2003 figures, so that the previous years are in proportion to the new rather than the old system. This means that for English, if enrollments had been tabulated in the new way in 2001–02, they would have been about 47,000 rather than 30,000; the 1998–1999 enrollments would have been about 38,000.

32. Only a quarter of these gains may be attributed to the new way of classifying "balanced combination" degree students after 2002-03. Today it is widely feared that the new scheme of funding and fees being imposed on British universities will siphon students out of the humanities into the sciences. But as Stefan Collini has pointed out, the altered financial incentives may in fact lead to a

further expansion of humanities courses, which are cheaper to run. Collini, "From Robbins to McKinsey," *LRB* 33 (25 August 2011): 9-14.

33. About 6% of the total US population (18 million of 300 million as of 2007) is currently enrolled in degree-granting institutions of one kind or another, versus about 3% in the United Kingdom. US Census Bureau, *Statistical Abstract of the United States 2011*, 178, Table 276: "Degree-Granting Institutions, Number and Enrollment by State: 2007."

34. Nationwide enrollment and graduation figures are based on summary tables from Statistics Canada: "University Enrolments by Registration Status and Sex, by Province," and "University Degrees, Diplomas and Certificates Granted, by Program Level and Instructional Program," 2006–2007. Higher education data are mainly gathered and published by individual provinces in Canada, according to their own counting and classificatory systems, with little coordination or reporting at the national level. My estimate for the number of English degree takers is extrapolated from the excellent statistical reports from Ontario, the largest of the provincial university systems with roughly 40% of the national enrollments. In 2002, Ontario graduated 56,864 undergraduates, of whom 2,136 were English majors (3.8%, almost identical to the US figure for that year). Allowing for Canada's 20% expansion of undergraduate enrollments between 2002 and 2007 (with the humanities growing faster than average), but also assuming that the share of degrees going to English majors may be lower in other provinces, particularly Quebec, we can conservatively guess 5,500 English degrees nationwide in 2007. See Tables 3.6.3a and 3.6.4 in *Facts and Figures 2006: A Compendium of Statistics on Ontario Universities*, at http://www.cou.on.ca.

35. Australian Government Department of Education, Employment and Workplace Relations, *Student 2009 Full Year: Selected Higher Education Statistics*, Award Course Completions, 2009, Table 1, "Award Course Completions for All Students by Citizenship and Level of Course 1998–2009," and Table 4.4, "Actual Student Load (EFTSL) for All Students by Narrow Discipline Group and Broad Level of Course."

36. Both the broad field of "Society and Culture" and the narrower one of "Language and Literature" have been expanding faster than

most other fields, and faster than the overall growth of domestic enrollments. Society and Culture continues to award the largest number of bachelor's degrees among domestic students, having expanded enrollments by nearly 70% since 1996. But the Australian higher education system has seen a stratospheric rise in international (mainly East Asian) students over the last decade, from 25,000 degree recipients in 1998 to nearly 100,000 in 2009, and more than three quarters of these students come to Australia to pursue degrees in business. This very narrowly oriented cohort has swollen the "Management and Commerce" numbers, which now exceed those for Society and Culture, even though the latter continues to be more popular and to grow more rapidly than the former among domestic students. Even with the foreign business students factored in, however, enrollments in Language and Literature programs are holding steady at about 3% of all bachelor's degree students: 16,840 or 2.9% in 2009 as against 15,500 or 3.0% in 2004. Australian Government Department of Education, Employment and Workplace Relations, *Student 2009 Full Year: Selected Higher Education Statistics*, Section 4, "All Student Load," Table 4.4: "Actual Student Load (EFTSL) for All Students by Narrow Discipline Group and Broad Level of Course"; and *Student 2009 Full Year Statistics, Award Course Completions 2009*, Table 3: "Award Course Completions for All Students by Citizenship and Broad Field of Education, 1998 to 2009," and Table 16: "Award Course Completions for Overseas Students by Level of Course, Broad Field of Education and Gender, 2009."

37. On the rising global demand for primary school teachers, see UNESCO Institute for Statistics, "Projecting the Global Demand for Teachers: Meeting the Goal of Universal Primary Education by 2015," Information Sheet No. 3 (Montreal: UNESCO, 2009).

38. Prior to the Bologna Process, launched in 1999 and aimed at assuring consistency and equivalency of degree programs across the European Higher Education Area, the "first degree" programs varied widely in terms of both nomenclature and required years of study. Today, more than a decade into the Bologna Process, we can speak meaningfully of bachelor's degree recipients in the Euro zone, and make coherent comparisons with their peers in Anglophone countries. Comparisons based on premillennial statistics are, however, necessarily shaky.

39. On the European roots of English studies, see Thomas Finkenstaedt and Gertrud Scholtes, eds., *Towards a History of English Studies in Europe* (Augsburg: University of Augsburg Press, 1983); and Balz Engler and Renate Haas, eds., *European English Studies: Contributions towards the History of a Discipline* (Leicester, UK: European Society for the Study of English, 2000). On the European origins of American studies, see Tim Watson, "Is the 'Post' in Postcolonial Studies the U.S. in American Studies? The U.S. Beginnings of Commonwealth Studies," *ARIEL: A Review of International English Literature* 31 (January–April 2000): 51–72. See also Martin A. Kayman, "Report on a Survey of English Studies in Europe at the Turn of the Century," sponsored by the European Society for the Study of English and the British Council, *The Messenger* (Spring 2005): http://www.essenglish.org/MAKreport.pdf.

40. The varying curricular complexion of English degree programs in Europe and their differences from degree programs elsewhere will be discussed in the third part of the book, but I will note here that the linguistic component is far more substantial for European English students (as also for those in South and East Asia) than for those in North America. The quotation from *EJES* is in Martin A. Kayman, Angela Locatelli, and Ansgar Nünning, "On Being 'European' in English," *European Journal of English Studies* 10 (April 2006): 3.

41. Kayman, "Report on a Survey of English Studies in Europe." While the percentage of students doing English as a combined degree, a minor, or a concentration within some other discipline is certainly much higher in Europe than in the United States, the latter has seen a pronounced tendency toward combined, multiple, or interdisciplinary degrees.

42. Imelda Bonel-Elliott, "English Studies in France," in Engler and Haas, *European English Studies*, 82.

43. Bonel-Elliott, "English Studies in France," 82.

44. Including the technical colleges, which constitute about half the postsecondary system in Greece, the GER rose from 27% in 1993 to 60% in 2004; if one counts only university enrollments, the ratio climbed from about 12% to 30%. Athanasios Kyriazis and Foteini Asderaki, *Higher Education in Greece*, Monographs on Higher Education (Bucharest: European Centre for Higher Education, 2008), Tables 47 and 48.

45. Post-secondary educational enrollments in Korea rose from about 200,000 in 1970 to 3.4 million in 2000; the country's GER had climbed to 66% by 1999, 94% in 2004, and 98% in 2009. *UNESCO Global Education Digest 2006* (Montreal: UNESCO Institute for Statistics) Table 8, 124; and *Global Education Digest 2010* (Montreal: UNESCO Institute for Statistics), Table 8, 164.

46. NCES, *Digest of Educational Statistics 2009*, Table 397: "Population, School Enrollment, and Teachers, by Major Areas of the World: Selected Years, 1980 through 2007." The figures in this table include all post-secondary enrollments, of which undergraduates in degree programs represent only a fraction. But the speed and scale of global expansion have not been much less among degree students.

47. Gauri Viswanathan, *Masks of Conquest: Literary Study and British Rule in India* (New York: Columbia University Press, 1989), 149–151.

48. Kailash C. Baral, "Postcoloniality, Critical Pedagogy, and English Studies in India," *Pedagogy: Critical Approaches to Teaching Literature, Language, Composition, and Culture* 6.13 (2006): 476, 477.

49. Braj B. Kachru, "World Englishes and Culture Wars," in Braj Kachru, Yamuna Kachru, and Cecil L. Nelson, eds., *The Handbook of World Englishes* (Oxford: Blackwell, 2006), 446.

50. Government data in India are notoriously unreliable and generally well out of date by the time they are reported. The official *All India Survey on Education* reports 15 million undergraduate and about half a million post-graduate enrollments for the most recent available year, 2007–08, similar to the 14.8 million total tertiary enrollments indicated for 2008 in UNESCO's *Global Education Digest 2010*, 168, Table 8. According to the Minister of Human Resource Development, there were 7.8 million full-time under-graduates enrolled in India's colleges and universities in 2004, which, if accurate, suggests that about a third of the total enroll-ments are part-time. These figures are roughly consistent with the estimate of 2 million degree takers in 2006, which comes from a report by the BBC. See Government of India, Ministry of Human Resource Development, Department of Higher Education, *Statistics of Higher & Technical Education 2008–09* (New Delhi: Bureau of Planning, Monitoring & Statistics, 2011), Table 3: "Enrolment (Excluding Open Universities) By Level/Courses (All Categories

of Students)"; "Undergraduate Enrollment in India (2000–2004): Question in the Lok Sabha," Unstarred Question Number 2221 (12 December 2004), available from the *Education in India* RSS feed, 24 May 2005. http://www.indiaedunews.net/rss/; and UNESCO Institute for Statistics Data Centre, Predefined Tables for Education, Table 15: "Enrolments by Broad Field of Education in Tertiary Education," http://stats.uis.unesco.org/unesco/TableViewer/tableView.aspx?ReportId=168.

51. According to the government's *Statistics of Higher & Technical Education 2008–09,* the number of affiliated and independent colleges exceeds 20,000, and there are an additional 7,500 certificate-granting vocational and teacher-training institutes that are not recognized as part of the higher educational system. *Renovation and Rejuvenation of Universities,* an interim report of the Committee to Advise on the Renovation and Rejuvenation of Higher Education (2009), available at http://www.academics-india.com/Yashpal%20Committee%20Report.doc, describes the failings of the many effectively vocational private institutions in the "colleges" category that should be reformed or reclassified.

52. For time-series gross enrollment ratios 1999–2008, see UNESCO Data Centre, Education Statistics, Table 14: "Tertiary Indicators." On GER trends in the Commonwealth countries, see Asha Kanwar and John Daniel, *The Scope and Demand for Tertiary Education and Current Resources Available to Commonwealth Member States,* Senior Officials Technical Working Group Meeting Proposal for a New Commonwealth Tertiary Education Facility (CTEF), 20 May (London: Commonwealth of Learning, 2008), http://www.col.org/SiteCollectionDocuments/Kanwar_JSD_080519CTEF_London.pdf.

53. "Renovation and Rejuvenation of Universities," 34.

54. For a statistical comparison of the two countries' systems, see Fengquiao Yan, *Indian Higher Education and Its Contribution to Economic Growth in Global and Knowledge Economy Era*, presentation at the Asian Development Bank 2008 annual meeting, Slide 4: "Table: Comparison Between India and China by Major Indicators in Tertiary Education," http://www.adb.org/annualmeeting/2008.

55. While the Chinese university system, like India's, has less in the way of financial resources than those in North America or Europe,

that gap is rapidly narrowing. If we look at expenditures on Research and Development, for example (an important indicator of public funding for higher education), China was spending 1.5% of its GDP in 2006, only about half of the United States' 3% and far less than some European countries. But this is triple the rate of just 10 years earlier, and China has set realistic goals of 2% in 2010 and 2.5% in 2020. The portion of its GDP being spent on higher education as a whole rose from 1% in 1998 to more than 4% in 2008, during which span China's GDP, currently the world's second largest, was growing at better than 5% per year. See OECD, *Education Policy Analysis: Focus on Higher Education 2005–06* (Paris: OECD, 2006), 52, Figure 1.18; and Jack Cheng, *Higher Education System in China – An Overview*, presentation at conference of the Asia Pacific Association for International Education and the European Association for International Education, Basel, 2006, http://www.economia.uniroma2.it/Public/YICGG/file/reading list/10/10_Jack_Cheng-Chinese_Higher_Edu-Overview-EAIE_APAIE.zip, slide 21.

56. Yao Li, "China's Higher Education Transformation and Its Global Implications," *Vox*, 18 April 2008, http://www.voxeu.org.

57. We should bear in mind that "tertiary" or "post-secondary" enrollments, as used for purposes of calculating GERs, include students enrolled in subdegree or vocational programs as well as in foreign institutions. Gross enrollment data for China include a large proportion of students studying at noncertified private institutions that do not confer regular college degrees. Even with the tremendous expansion of the state-certified higher educational apparatus in China, consumer demand, supported by fast-rising discretionary budgets among the emerging middle classes, has vastly outstripped supply – and private minibans have proliferated to sop up the excess. Gerard Postiglione, director of the Centre for the Study of Education in China at the University of Hong Kong, estimated in 2001 that only one third of all tertiary enrollments were students in certified undergraduate degree programs. Postiglione, "China's Expansion, Consolidation, and Globalization," *International Higher Education* 24 (Summer 2001): 10–12. That ratio appears to have come down somewhat over the past decade, since China's 3 million annual degree takers suggest a current degree-seeking population of 12–14 million within a total tertiary population of about 30

million. In any case, there is no doubt that the growth of China's certified university system has been the fastest in the world. A good analytical snapshot of tertiary education in China is provided by Kathryn Mohrman, director of the Hopkins-Nanjing Center: "The Emerging Global Model with Chinese Characteristics," *Higher Education Policy* 21 (2008): 29–48.

58. Colleagues in China have tracked down for me what they regard as the most reliable estimates, as summarized in a 2009 article by a noted expert on foreign language studies in China, Wenzhong Hu of Beijing Foreign Studies University; see Wenzhong Hu, "The Strengths and Weaknesses of China's Foreign Language Education in the Past 60 Years," *Foreign Language Teaching and Research*, 41.3 (2009): 163–169. Hu notes that one of the weaknesses of foreign language and literature studies in China is the lack of good statistics, which hampers efforts to recognize and institute needed reforms (168). But he cites a 2008 study by Dai Weidong that found "nearly 1,000 English departments" in China's colleges and universities, compared with 385 Japanese departments, 70 German and French departments, and 14 Spanish departments (166). And he cites another 2008 study, by Liu Daoyi, that estimates "about 500,000 undergraduate English majors in Chinese colleges and universities" (166). The article as well as the studies cited in it are available only in Chinese; I am grateful to Hu Jing of Nanjing University for researching and translating. Among studies available in English, I have relied on the figures provided in Junyue Chang, "Research Report: Globalization and English in Chinese Higher Education," *World Englishes* 25.3–4 (2006): 517. There are also the data reported in the 2009 university rankings at http://www.echinacities.com, which show more than 9% of college graduates taking degrees in literature: more than a quarter million a year. For purposes of the charts and comparisons in this book, I am conservatively estimating 75,000 English bachelor's degrees in China each year; the actual figure could be twice that.

59. The 15- to 19-year-old population peaked in 2005 at 117 million, and is expected to bottom out at 85 million in 2020. However, the demand for places continues to outstrip by a huge margin the capacity of China's university system. See Geoff Maslen, "Chinese Students to Dominate World Market," *University World News* 4 (4 November 2007): 40.

Part II

The Future of English Professors

*Efficiency versus Prestige
in the Age of Global Rankings*

The Economics of Massification

While the current global enrollment boom does in many respects put the lie to doomsday rhetorics about English's future, it is obvious that not all the features of this educational expansion are benign. A rapidly rising tide can do more damage than a receding one, tearing more violently at stable foundations and long-standing boundaries. Even if the gradual drifting away of English majors as described by the prophets of our discipline's "slow death" is largely a mirage, perhaps its correlate, the ever-narrowing employment prospects and eroding job conditions for teachers of college-level English studies, is for real. Isn't it true that most of the secure and well-compensated faculty positions in English are being carved out of the world's academic system, leaving gaps and fissures to be filled with whatever degraded forms of instructional labor can be most cheaply and conveniently obtained?

Here again, the short answer is no: the worldwide massification of higher ed is creating more good faculty jobs as well as more bad ones. Even in the United States, which has been aggressively degrading and casualizing academic labor since the 1970s, there

The Global Future of English Studies, First Edition. James F. English.
© 2012 John Wiley & Sons, Ltd. Published 2012 by John Wiley & Sons, Ltd.

are 25% more tenured or tenure-track faculty than there were 30 years ago, and average full-time faculty salaries have been rising throughout that period, gaining against both inflation and median income.[1] Globally, there is no question that the de facto tenured professoriate in English is larger today than at any time in its history.[2] China alone is producing a huge number of new tenurable positions.[3] Secure and good-paying jobs that involve scholarly research and writing as well as teaching not only are not merely vestigial anachronisms in the global higher educational system, they remain an intrinsic feature without which the system cannot function.

These points need to be emphasized, as they are routinely left out of our crisis narratives. But the anxieties that feed those narratives are not unwarranted. As with the surge of enrollments in the world's English degree programs, the expansion of the faculty in English involves a divergence between (rising) absolute and (declining) relative numbers, a widening of disparities between the system's winners and losers, and some highly uneven developments across the world's educational landscapes. The overall picture with respect to academic work — as with respect to labor generally in the "global" age — is not a pretty one. But nor is it, for the professoriate in English, a simple document of our extinction.[4]

It may be necessary to remind ourselves at the outset that the drive to extend higher educational access to a majority of the world's population never implied a simple scaling up of what was traditionally an elite system for the wealthy centered on a research faculty in the liberal arts. In the early 1960s, often invoked as a kind of golden age for English professors in Britain, the British university system enrolled barely 4% of the college-age population.[5] There was never a moment when the world was tending toward accommodation of several hundreds of thousands of English professors enjoying 6- or 8-hour teaching loads, regular sabbaticals, and professional-level salaries to support their independent (and in itself largely nonremunerative) reading and writing. Not even in today's most popular and institutionally valorized disciplines — business, engineering, and health sciences — is the traditional research professor, as invented in nineteenth-century Germany, a viable model for mass instruction. The levels of subsidization required to build and maintain such a faculty, however desirable it might be, were never envisioned except in the most naïve fantasies of the professoriate itself. Worldwide, the average income per person ($6000) is barely a fifth of what the United States spends per university student per year, and not even a tenth of what is spent on a student at Columbia or Princeton or the other institutions where faculty are most comfortably employed (and where faculty compensation alone costs several times more per student than the world average income).[6] Eighty percent of the world's people fall below that average income level; there are many dozens of countries where the percentage whose income is above the world average can be measured in single digits. Even in the United States and the other richest countries, few can actually afford the cost of a leading university without subsidy, since more than half the income and nearly all wealth in those countries are concentrated in the hands of just 20% of the population.[7] That wealthiest one fifth of the people in the richest countries, who represent just a few percent of the total world population and who, prior to massification, would have constituted the entire universe of higher education, remain the core constituency for the world's top-ranked and best endowed colleges and universities. Such institutions serve this elite fraction not as engines of democracy but rather as highly effective machines for preserving social advantage, and the massification of academe has if anything intensified their counter-democratizing effects.

This is perhaps most readily evident in the United States, where the drive toward mass higher education had an earlier start than elsewhere. What has happened during the decades of steadily rising rates of enrollment is that the US university system has become *more* rigidly stratified and *more* reinforcing of economic advantage, with fewer and fewer students from moderate- and low-income families attending Ivy League and other leading institutions.[8] Admissions data from Oxford and Cambridge indicate a similar hardening of hierarchies in the United Kingdom during the more recent push toward mass enrollment there (from just 12% of the college-age population in 1980 to nearly half today).[9] Research conducted in other countries gives us no reason to view this as anything other than a normative pattern. As Bourdieu and Passeron argued long ago, higher education tends (on balance, in the aggregate, but with many individual exceptions) to legitimate social power by euphemizing it as intellectual merit.[10] The massification of this system implies only an extension of its efficacy; it does not involve any redirection of the system to assure gains in social equity.[11]

What a mass education academy, an academy for the majority of the relevant-age population in all the countries of the world, does have to assure, however, is higher education that is overall less expensive on a per-student basis than an elite one, with very large and/or numerous low-cost institutions widening out the base beneath a small, established, and relatively stable upper tier of much costlier ones. Faculty at the new or fast-expanding institutions – the two-year public community colleges in United States, the post-1992 New Universities in the United Kingdom (the former polytechnics and colleges of higher education), the local colleges and distance universities in China, and the for-profit bottom-feeding institutions that have been proliferating nearly everywhere – are on average less well paid and receive less support for their research than those at the established institutions, where enrollment has tended to be more stable. The disproportionate role of these newer institutions in academe's massification corresponds with a downward tendency in the overall standards of qualification, compensation, and working conditions for the faculty. This is not to excuse the particular forms of degradation that academic labor has undergone in the United States or elsewhere, nor to deny the rampant casualization of teaching and gouging of instructor salaries at even the wealthiest and most prestigious institutions. These matters will be discussed further below. The point is simply that the growth of higher education was never a promise of comparable growth of the traditional professoriate. On the contrary, massification has assured that the best kinds of faculty job, the well-compensated, tenured professorships that evolved in the system of modern research universities in Europe and North America, become a smaller fraction of the instructional workforce as a whole. Other and more pernicious factors have intensified and accelerated that process, even to the point where in a number of countries we have reason to hope that it is butting up against structural limits and beginning to meet effective forms of resistance. But in the meantime, we should not mistake the relative shrinkage of our tenured research and teaching faculty as equivalent to their disappearance (as suggested by the rhetoric of "the last professors," "the last good job," etc.), nor even as the curtailment of their power to affect the shape of the discipline's future. On the contrary, the global massification of academia presents this advantaged fraction of the faculty with some urgent challenges and responsibilities, particularly, for those of us in English studies, with respect to our dysfunctional systems of apprenticeship and publication.

Doing More with Less

As they respond to the global mandate for higher GERs with ever more ambitious enrollment and retention targets, most countries have had to enlarge their faculties significantly. The total post-secondary instructional workforce grew by 50% between 1995 and 2005, representing about 3 million new teaching jobs over and above replacements.[12] (See Figure 2.1.) Yet even this impressive recruitment of new faculty could not nearly keep pace with the drive toward mass higher education. Over the same 10-year period, tertiary enrollments grew by some 95%, nearly twice as fast as the faculty.[13] (See Figure 2.2.) These statistics help to quantify what we already know about the academic workplace: that it is being retooled for greater "efficiency," with the managers of higher education (whether public, private, or part of the expanding system of public-private alliances) attempting to extract more and more instruction per instructor. Or, to express this in the standard language of crisis, we are faced with "a global crisis of rising demand

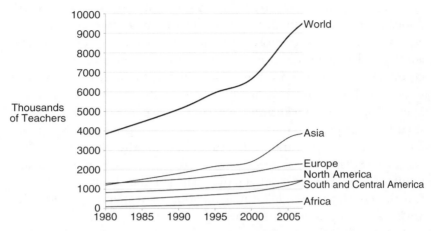

Figure 2.1   Number of teachers in tertiary education, 1980–2007, selected regions.

Source: National Center for Education Statistics, *Digest of Education Statistics* 2009, Table 397; adapted by NCES from UNESCO, *Statistical Yearbook* 1999; and unpublished tabulations.

for higher education which races ahead of the public funding to meet it."[14]

Owing in part to inconsistent definitions of "teacher" as well as of "post-secondary," "tertiary," and "higher" education, it can be misleading to compare reported student-teacher ratios across national borders. But according to UNESCO's Institute for Education Statistics (which in general estimates higher ratios than the NCES data represented in Figure 2.2), there are a few countries, including Canada, Mexico, and Japan, which have managed over the past two decades to keep their student-to-teacher ratios impressively low (9, 10, and 11, respectively). Most countries, however, have been creeping upward from an average of below 15 in the early 1990s toward an average of 18 in 2008: though still only 16 in the United States, it is now 18 in the United Kingdom and France, 19 in Australia, and 22 in Italy. And countries where enrollment growth has been most rapid are stretched even further: in 2006 there were 23 students per teacher in China,

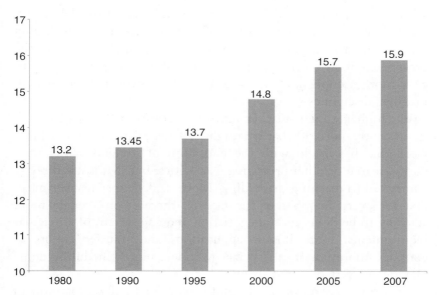

Figure 2.2   Student–teacher ratio in tertiary education worldwide, 1980–2007.

Source: National Center for Education Statistics, *Digest of Higher Education Statistics* 2009, Table 398.

a ratio nearly 75% higher than in 1994 despite the government's massive post-millennial investment in higher education and its concerted effort to improve quality as well as broaden access. In India, where the state has provided much less adequate funding for the enrollment boom, opening new universities without in some cases sufficient budgets to hire even half the needed instructors, the student–teacher ratio has climbed to 26.[15]

These rising ratios obviously result in either higher teaching loads (more courses per instructor) or more crowded classrooms (more students per course). In the latter case, distance learning, with its easily scalable virtual classrooms, holds a distinct advantage. Britain's Open University has nearly 50% more students per teacher than the national average; one distance institution in China enrolls more than a million students in just 600 courses, with a student-to-faculty ratio, by its own count, of 1000:1.[16] But whatever means are used to achieve these higher ratios, the faculty must shoulder a heavier burden of instructional labor, including the assessment and grading of student work, which, owing to the greater emphasis on the particulars of written expression, tends to be a more arduous and time-consuming process in English than in other disciplines.

But higher student–teacher ratios also confront the faculty with significantly more of what we might call "para-instructional labor": work that has to do with the education of students rather than with research or other professional activities, but that is not directly connected to teaching or grading. More students per teacher mean that for every member of the faculty, there is on average more advising to be done, more negotiation and adjustment of curricular requirements, more honors applications and transfer credits to consider, more honors and prizes to judge, more scheduling complexities to sort out, and so on.

This further expansion of faculty workloads, the expansion of para-instructional work, has been greatly compounded by the casualization of the instructional workforce. As we know, the global pressure to expand access has led the higher educational systems not only to let rising enrollments outpace faculty hiring, but also to concentrate what hiring they do undertake on less expensive, short-contract and, especially, part-time instructors, a cost control strategy that has been pursued in the United States since the early 1970s but is of relatively recent advent elsewhere.

It is important not to misrepresent the aggregate employment situation, in which the dramatic expansion of academe as a whole has permitted *both* the extensive casualization of instructional labor *and* an increase in the number of tenured or effectively permanent full-time teaching and research positions. The standard doomsday rhetoric about English professors, and higher educational faculty more generally, obscures the fact that the absolute number of such traditional professorial positions, and even the number of such positions per capita, has been rising in most countries.[17] In France, to take one example, the full-time, permanent academic faculty has doubled in size since the mid-1980s.[18]

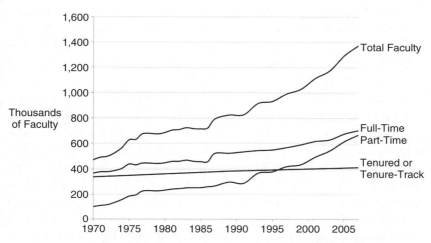

Figure 2.3 Number of instructional faculty by employment status, United States, 1970–2007.

Source: National Center for Education Statistics, *Digest of Education Statistics* 2009, Table 249; and AAUP *Contingent Faculty Index* 2006.

But these "gold standard" jobs account for only a fraction of the overall growth of the academic workforce.[19] In the United States, where the drive toward a more contingent professoriate has been underway for 40 years, the percentage of faculty who were outside the tenure stream was already 58% in 1995, and by 2005 it had risen to 68%, despite the fact that the tenure stream itself was becoming more populous in these years. The ranks of part-time faculty grew during the same period from 41% to 48%, and today part-timers almost certainly constitute a majority of American academics.[20] Figure 2.3 shows the overall tendency toward casualization across the entire post-secondary system since the 1970s.[21] Though the percentages differ significantly in other countries, the general trend is observable nearly everywhere. It is worst of all in the universities of South and Latin America, where dramatic enrollment growth has led to aggressive faculty hiring on the cheap, with nearly 80% of the faculty now consisting of part-time, "taxi-cab" instructors.[22] Even in Chinese universities, which have created hundreds of thousands of new, permanent, full-time faculty positions in the last decade and where the use of part-time faculty is comparatively rare, the part-time fraction has roughly tripled since the mid-1990s, from 8.5% of the teaching staff in 1996 to more than 22% in 2005.[23]

It has been shown that part-time faculty in the United States, who earn barely a quarter of what tenure-line faculty are paid on a per-course basis, are not able to devote as much time to the out-of-classroom aspects of teaching and learning.[24] This is as one might expect, and the finding could presumably be generalized to other countries. The part-time faculty are after all neither paid nor expected to act as members of an intellectual and pedagogical "community"; they are afforded little or no role in institutional governance or administration; and in most cases they are not even provided adequate office facilities for preparing classes or meeting with students. From the standpoint of the university that employs them, part-time faculty are cut-rate piecework laborers, hired to convene specific (mostly lower-level) classes at the appointed hour, submit grade sheets at the end of term, and wait to hear whether they are needed the following semester. In most cases, rising enrollments have meant a strong likelihood of continued employment, but adjunct instructors lack the very high level of job security that virtually all regular, full-time faculty enjoy even in the many countries, such as the United Kingdom, where there is no formal system of tenure and no legal guarantee of permanent employment.[25] There are a few countries (Italy being the most prominent) where part-time status carries no implication of contingency and extends to many permanent members of the senior professoriate.[26] But these are merely exceptions that prove the rule: a more part-time workforce is a more contingent workforce. In the United Kingdom, for example, part-time academic staff are nearly three times more likely than full-time academic staff to be on fixed-term contract.[27] And since few universities pay their part-time faculty a living wage, this kind of labor often involves juggling multiple teaching jobs or teaching on top of a primary job in a different profession. In either case, the hours of availability on campus must be pared to the minimum.

As a consequence of these conditions and constraints facing part-time instructors, the increasing para-instructional workload (including, at some institutions, the rising workload involved in hiring and assessing all these part-time, short-contract instructors) falls disproportionately on the tenure-line faculty, whose continuing advantages of employment tend to veil the strains they face as a shrinking fraction of an ever larger and more demanding enterprise.[28] They, too, are expected to "do more with less" – not, in this case, more teaching with less job security and compensation, but more para-instructional labor with less of a tenure-stream cohort to share the burden. Not surprisingly, studies show that as the proportion of full-time, tenure-line faculty decreases at a given institution, they become less attentive and effective as individual teachers, advisers, and mentors to the students in their program.[29]

The drive toward greater productivity and efficiency, in other words, is actually producing a distracted faculty that faces more and more in the way of para-instructional labor, which it is performing less and less thoroughly and responsibly. Another inter-related development has been the pronounced growth of bureaucratic tasks and paperwork observable in all the disciplines and across every form and level of educational institution. Alongside the increasing casualization of instructional staff and the burgeoning of provostial, decanal, subdecanal, and other administrative offices, this is felt by the faculty as a kind of malign yet unstoppable force of nature. But it is a directly intentional effect of late-capitalist managerialism, which has taken firm hold as the governing ideology of the so-called emerging global model (EGM) of the research university.[30] The business-managerialist conception of academe is not exactly new; absent the "global" dimension, it has been a strong force in American educational debates since the late nineteenth century. But over the last quarter century it has taken a new global-neoliberal form and become for the first time truly hegemonic, part of the uncontested doxa or common sense of academic administration. For administrators, in the ever more privatized public sector as well as in the private sector itself, academic managerialism not only sets an agenda of (financial) rationalization but also provides a rationale for its own expansion in numbers and disproportionate increases in salary.[31] The expanding bureaucratic workload, which they themselves are imposing, ostensibly justifies the larger and larger share of university budgets that they themselves are consuming.[32]

The implementation of this new managerialist common sense was especially rapid and dramatic in the United Kingdom, where a decisive shift was effected during the third term of the Thatcher government and the early years of New Labour. Institutions were suddenly forced to compete more directly with one another, while at the same time being subject to far more scrutiny and control from the central government, whose role was to organize and orchestrate the whole competitive marketplace in such a way as to "bring higher educational institutions closer to the world of business" (as it was expressed in the Thatcher government's "Meeting the Challenge" White Paper of 1987).[33] This blending of the market competition model with the state control model (actually more characteristic of "Third Way" New Labourism than of Thatcherite free marketism) depended on a new overarching scheme of accountability and assessment, which quickly produced in the United Kingdom a staggering demand for documentation and quantification of educational inputs and outputs. Over the years, these bureaucratic tasks associated with "continuous assessment" of every unit at every level have come to consume more and more faculty time – to the point where, according to one recent study, lecturers in Wales are now devoting an average of 25 hours a week to them.[34]

In the United Kingdom, as elsewhere, this was from the outset a global rather than a strictly national development. A good part of the impetus for such reforms, as for the entire neoliberal agenda, was the state's special emphasis on global competitiveness. The national higher education system had to be made internally more competitive and business-like in order to contend in an external competition against the systems of all other countries:

for maximum access, maximum efficiency, maximum achievement, and maximum attractiveness to the fast-growing ranks of mobile international education consumers (for whom Britain is the leading destination after the United States, and China its biggest source of student-customers).[35] And of course this international-market aspect of the model increased still further the demand for documentation and quantitative or quasi-quantitative assessment, introducing a wider scope of study and comparison.

Despite its manifest tendency to draw both money and faculty instructional time away from students (not to mention any deleterious qualitative effects on research and writing), this "paperwork paradigm" of detailed reporting and continuous assessment has become the model for most of the world's educational systems. Even though post-secondary educational expansion has occurred disproportionately in the scattered interstices of the private sector, with rapid proliferation nearly everywhere outside Western Europe of the kinds of small, local, private institutions that are not readily susceptible to centralized management, the new managerialism has established itself as the norm. From all corners of the academic world we find similarly unhappy field reports. In Hong Kong and elsewhere in East Asia, for example, scholars have observed rapid "growth in total managerial and administrative work at institutional and intra-institutional level" and a consequent rise of "paperwork and administrative tasks" throughout their educational systems. They find themselves operating within a global horizon of "academic capitalism" that is effecting a worldwide "bureaucratization of the collegium."[36]

Demand for the Doctorate

It is doubtful that these broad and interlocking tendencies in higher education – more students per instructor, more part-time and short-contract instructors per tenure-stream faculty position, more para-instructional labor and assessment-driven paperwork per student-hour of instruction, and more dependence on the private sector – are biting more sharply into English studies than other disciplines. The actual number of regular, full-time, de facto tenured, or tenurable faculty positions in English continues to grow worldwide, albeit far more slowly than student enrollments. Anecdotal evidence suggests that in the countries facing severe shortages of capable English instructors, even the contingent positions are in some cases offering more attractive compensation and benefits than in the past. In the United States, on the other hand, English is one of the disciplines in which there has been actual faculty contraction, with tenured or tenurable positions eroding away at the rate of about 1% per year since the early 1990s, and short-contract or adjunct positions not emerging quite rapidly enough to compensate fully for this shrinkage.[37] Newly graduated PhDs in English can expect to spend years, often futilely, seeking tenure-track employment. Their plight, perhaps more than any other single factor, is what leads US scholars to conclude that English is facing more dire prospects than most other disciplines.

Yet even here there is room to view the situation from a different perspective than that of the slow-death hypothesis. With respect to employment no less than enrollments, it is an error to use the brief spike of the late 1960s as a standard and to continue retailing narratives of contraction and decline based on that misleading chapter. We have had nearly 40 years to adjust to the discipline's sudden fall-back to normal levels, and over that span the number of advertised beginning tenure-track positions in English has hovered around a mean of about 800, with pronounced surges and declines of up to 50% in either direction (including the recent brutal contraction following the crash of 2008), but with no overall trend either upward or downward.[38] Eight hundred thus represents a sustainable annual target figure.

Or rather, it stands as an indicator of a target that in the short run is much lower. Though on average about 800 vacant assistant professorships of English are filled each year, the successful applicants for those jobs include many candidates who took their PhDs in earlier years but are either still looking for tenurable employment or are hoping to upgrade or relocate from an existing tenure-track position. The Association of Departments of English estimates that the market can absorb only about 500 newly graduated PhDs each year, though that number would climb higher, to about 700, if the reservoir of underemployed and unemployed PhDs from earlier years were drained down.[39]

So the real number of tenurable positions open to new PhDs in English is in the range of 500–700 a year, and, allowing for sharp fluctuations, this median figure has not changed for decades. Of course, a steady state of demand is nothing to celebrate. The demographics of enrollment and retirement would have predicted a long and strong wave of tenure-track hiring in English, but this would-be boom has been offset by the casualization of the workforce and (to a lesser extent) the increasing of student-teacher ratios in English classes. In this sense, Marc Bousquet, a leading voice for academic workers, is perfectly right to say that the demand for tenure-track English professors has been "artificially suppressed" and that the whole hiring system has been rigged in such a way as to preclude normal business cycles and assure that no "boom" will ever follow the long bust.[40] Still, the upshot has been a stable if low demand for new assistant professors of English holding doctoral degrees.

Despite the immiseration faced by many of the students to whom we have conferred PhDs, we have refused to accept this strategically suppressed but stable limit. The collective US graduate programs in English have consistently produced more PhDs than can be justified by our placement results, preferring to scorn the ideology of the market and its strategic artifices than to craft a market strategy of our own.[41] We give our individual students all kinds of advice about how to make themselves more impressive and alluring to prospective employers, how to beat the competition as individual self-marketers, but we take no collective steps to manage the number of degree recipients in ways that would afford all the graduates greater agency within the profession. This posture of market refusal, from which we can pretend that because the academic job market is part of a cynical system for maintaining the contingent labor force (which it is), we cannot affect it by altering the scale of our graduate programs (which we can), plays well into the hands of our employers and managers.[42] It not only reduces the odds that our PhD graduates will find full-time tenurable employment, but exerts steady downward pressure on the compensation and job security for all faculty in the discipline, assuring that salaries will be on average lower and contracts more stringent than in other fields. (Just the opposite conditions have been in effect in business and management, where the number of PhDs graduating from US business schools declined 12% between 1995 and 2005 even while demand for faculty, both domestically and globally, was surging. Starting salaries for tenure-track business faculty are now more than double the salaries for starting assistant professors in English, and while the use of part-time faculty is no less pronounced in the business schools – "flexibility," after all, is an MBA watchword – the terms of adjunct employment are less insulting.)[43]

There was a moment, in the mid- to late 1980s, when this irrationality in English doctoral programs seemed to be waning. Having produced more than 1900 new PhDs in 1973, the profession had gradually whittled that number down by 50%, to a much more reasonable level of about 900–1000 a year between 1983 and 1990, with a low of 853 in 1987.[44] Given that roughly 20% of those who earn PhDs are not interested in pursuing full-time professorial careers, this figure was close to the target.[45] With less overproduction, the backlog of job seekers from earlier years began to shrink, so that more and more of the new graduates were finding tenure-track employment straight away; a market, that in 1983 was so backed up with past degree recipients it could not even absorb 300 new PhDs, was absorbing nearly 500 by decade's end. From about 1987 to 1991, English enjoyed a relatively balanced doctoral job market, with nearly all the new PhDs who wanted professorial careers able to find tenurable employment within 2 years.[46] The desperate situation of our graduate students was in the process of becoming significantly less so, and if we had maintained control over the size of our doctoral programs, holding fast at or below the level of 1988, the state of play today would be far more palatable than it is.[47] But, encouraged by successful placements, the doctoral programs had already by then begun admitting significantly more students – a trend that was boosted by publication in 1989 of the so-called Bowen Report, with its ill-conceived and wildly overoptimistic view of the "Prospects for Faculty in the Arts and Sciences."[48] By 1993, the number of new PhD recipients had climbed back to over 1200; 5 years later, despite a hiring trough in the early 1990s, the figure had reached nearly 1500; and it has been averaging about 1300 ever since.[49]

Of course, it is a simplification to say that "we" in the English departments have failed to exercise restraint in the scaling of our doctoral programs, since the size of degree programs is ultimately controlled by a university's administration. The growth of graduate programs in English can be attributed in part to the universities' increasing and exploitative employment of graduate student teaching assistants (TAs) as cut-rate teachers, especially teachers of first-year writing classes and lower-level literature classes. Doctoral students form a more crucial part of the pool of adjunct instructors in English than in most other disciplines. At the wealthiest institutions, where all entering English PhD students receive multi-year tuition-plus-stipend fellowship packages worth as much as $300,000 over the span of the degree program, where average time to completion and cumulative attrition rates are comparatively low, and where students do relatively little teaching, there is no financial advantage to the university in expanding graduate admissions.[50] And in fact, the English PhD programs at schools like Princeton and Stanford tend to be slightly smaller today than they were 20 years ago. But the vast majority of institutions, including those with the largest doctoral programs and the lowest rates of completion (i.e., the largest numbers of nominally "student" employees who never in fact receive a degree), extract far more instructional labor from their graduate students than they pay for in the form of fellowship support and tuition waivers. Most students are supported by "teaching assistantships" that provide stipends on the order of just $3,000 per course, which is even less than the already obscenely low national market rate for part-time instructors. And since they are classified as students, they not only provide the university with a cheap and reliable supply of instructional labor, but also occupy a conveniently euphemized position within the larger workforce – albeit not an altogether docile one (witness their important role in the academic labor movement).

Although this arrangement has often been fostered by administrators, the tenured English faculties have made no collective effort to resist it and have in fact lent their own energies to sustaining it. This is partly because we'd rather have graduate students teaching first-year writing classes than be stuck teaching them ourselves. Both PhD-granting English departments and baccalaureate-only departments typically assign about 55% of their freshman writing classes to contingent and part-time faculty. But whereas in the doctoral departments, virtually all the remaining sections are handled by graduate student TAs, in the baccalaureate departments that obligation rests entirely on the tenure-stream faculty.[51]

But as most tenured faculty at research universities must recognize, their instructional role with respect to writing classes is not really dependent on the precise size of their PhD program. In departments that already have a graduate program, a 30% contraction of doctoral admissions (as required to gain any leverage over the tenure-stream placement rate) would not force more tenured faculty into composition classrooms; it would rather lead to an expansion of the adjunct faculty. This, too, could conceivably have negative practical implications for the standing faculty, who would bear at least some of the annual para-instructional burden of hiring, training, and evaluating the adjunct instructors, and who might find that graduate students in other disciplines – history, philosophy, and communications – began stepping into the instructional void, effecting a transfer of enrollments and budget from English into other departments. As English department chairs have long recognized, there are material advantages to keeping composition enrollments in house, provided there are young apprentices around to handle the concomitant chores.

But the main reasons why tenured faculty have colluded in the overproduction of PhDs are not so much practical as symbolic.

There is after all status to be derived from teaching and advising at the graduate level; a professor's CV often proudly lists the dissertations directed, and as with publications and awards, the more the better. Many of us routinely fight to admit more graduate students in our particular area of specialization, thereby collectively assuring constant pressure from below for expansion of the doctoral cohort. If my field of expertise is a marginal or imperiled one (and whose isn't?), I can rationalize this agitation as serving a wider intellectual cause: the educational world needs more teachers and scholars in my field either because that field is struggling to emerge (Latina poetry; the digital book) or because it is struggling to survive (Old English prose; eighteenth-century drama). Either way, the imperatives of this struggle trump any concern I might have for the imbalance of the national tenure-stream job market.

We fail to take the measure of the gains that could be won by correcting that imbalance. Yes, we would have fewer graduate students to work with, but by way of compensatory status rewards, those we did work with would generally enjoy superior career trajectories. They would enter our programs through a more selective admissions process and would exit with more attractive employment options. The escalating pressures of what John Guillory has called "preprofessionalization" – employers' (and advisers') demands for ever longer CVs, and more and more publications and conference papers – would be somewhat lessened as the baseline credential for tenurable research faculty itself became rarer.[52] Even those who took part-time positions could expect to earn more than at present for their teaching, since the employing university would have a smaller pool of similarly qualified labor to draw from.

In addition to recalibrating our own demands regarding graduate teaching, we can advance this agenda of doctoral down-sizing by supporting the graduate instructors' collective demands for higher wages and more comprehensive benefits. As long as graduate students are the cheapest pool of instructional labor a university has at its disposal, the incentives will be skewed in favor of oversized doctoral programs. It is in our general interest to drive up the cost of graduate labor and/or to increase nonservice fellowship support while reducing the teaching component of graduate degree programs to the minimum required for purposes of professional mentoring and development (perhaps 4–6 courses during the 4–6 years of academic fellowship support). Whatever teaching students might do over and above this minimum they would do as workers, not as students. Their status in that capacity – as "graduate employees" – should be contractually recognized and their labor compensated accordingly, at the level of a living wage with benefits. These are not goals that can be achieved as long as tenured faculty stand on the sidelines of the academic labor movement, much less if they actively oppose it.

★   ★   ★

What I have been sketching is obviously a limited, national strategy rather than a global one. While there are increasing currents of international flow in the academic workforce, they mainly operate above or below the level of the beginning tenure-track professor: either in the market for senior faculty or in the recruitment of graduate students (many of whom eventually seek employment in the country of their degree program rather than that of their citizenship). In English as in other disciplines, the market for entry-level faculty positions is still by and large a local one. One needs therefore to exercise considerable caution when speaking about global supply or global demand for PhDs. There does appear to be a glut of English doctorates in the other established Anglophone education systems (United Kingdom, Australia, and Canada), much as there is in the United States. But in many countries, and especially those where enrollment growth has been most rapid, there are signs of serious shortages. In China and India, where tertiary enrollments have doubled or tripled in the space of a few years, MA and PhD production is lagging far behind the educational systems' apparent needs. Institutions seeking to hire new faculty with research degrees are unable to do so, and many advertised positions go unfilled, or are filled with personnel who

72

lack the normal credentials. In China's tertiary system, to offer one quick example, only 9% of faculty possess a PhD, and there are many instructors at unaccredited private colleges and remote local universities in China who lack even a bachelor's degree.[53]

But does this mean that, beyond the horizon of traditional Anglophone English departments, there is a need for many more PhDs? One of the most authoritative scholars of international higher education, Philip G. Altbach, has described the problem of inadequate faculty qualifications not simply in terms of market shortage but also as a systemic and cynical slackening of standards, a worldwide "dumbing down of the Professoriate."[54] The implicit warning in this analysis is that attempts to reverse the downward slide by improving the world's academic market conditions – bringing the supply of PhDs up to meet the demand caused by burgeoning enrollments – would be to fall for a global version of the Bowen Report's misleading projections. After all, we have seen in our own educational system that the scale of the traditional (degree-holding, tenure-stream) professoriate is not at all correlative with the burden of instructional labor; more work doesn't mean more professors. The system's managers see degradation or dumbing down of the instructional workforce in terms of gains in efficiency. Throwing more PhDs into this mix can make matters worse rather than better.

And yet, Altbach and other scholars of academic globalization do endorse a global push for more and larger graduate programs, figuring that countries which are still early in the process of massification really do face severe shortages in the supply of qualified faculty. They conclude that on balance the demand for professors holding research degrees – in English as in other fields – will be rising for the foreseeable future. But it *is* a question of balance, of a divided agenda in the global academy, which tends on the one side toward higher efficiency via the erosion of baseline credentials, and on the other side toward higher status via the accumulation of symbolic capital.

The negative tendency, which is increasing the ratio of students to PhD-holding faculty worldwide, has two main components.

First, there is the fact that rapid enrollment growth always occurs disproportionately at the kinds of institutions – technical colleges, local commuter universities, the small, often family-owned for-profit colleges in India and other Asian countries, and the "new universities" in the United Kingdom – where faculty are not expected to hold higher research degrees (and may even be viewed with suspicion if they do). During the period of fastest expansion in the US higher education system, the 1960s and 1970s, public two-year community colleges grew much faster than other institutions, with new campuses opening at the rate of one per week and enrollments climbing tenfold, from 11% of the total postsecondary population in 1960 to 35% of the total in 1979.[55] Yet in comparison with 4-year institutions, and especially with research universities, community colleges employ very few PhDs. Less than 20% of their full-time faculty holds that degree versus 75% of the faculty at research universities.[56] The institutions that emerge to absorb the surging popular demand for access are after all primarily teaching institutions, not research institutions. A strong case can be made that even these teaching colleges should employ faculty capable of understanding and applying new research in their field, and that minimum faculty qualifications should be geared to that level. But it is to be expected that as we move outward from the most advanced research universities to the more informal and vocational sectors of mass tertiary education, the perceived need for doctoral-trained faculty decreases.

The other factor that works against the rising demand for PhDs is of course casualization, and especially the rising ratios of part-time to full-time faculty. In the United States, part-time faculty are only about a third as likely to hold the doctorate as their full-time colleagues, and this ratio is even lower in other countries. These two factors are mutually reinforcing inasmuch as the tendency for student enrollments to amass in those zones of the educational system where PhDs are scarcest also puts them precisely where part-time faculty are traditionally most prevalent. Unfortunately, as we have seen, part-time faculty are becoming more prevalent everywhere, so this part of the doctoral-demand picture represents a potentially more profound problem for the aspiring future professoriate. It is one thing to recognize that massification involves proportional redistribution (a rising percentage of students in lower tier institutions), ensuring that most of the increased instructional workload falls outside the sphere where PhD-holding faculty are the norm. It is quite another thing to contemplate that latter sphere itself in a state of continual erosion, the professoriate subject to a decredentialing process without end.

But, as I said, there are in fact counter-tendencies which are pushing the demand for faculty with research degrees in a positive direction, even despite casualization. Again, the situation in the United States, though far from typical in its particulars, helps to illuminate the general logic of massification and managerialism. Looking at data from 1993 and 2003, we find that the increasing reliance on part-time faculty has not in fact brought down the percentage of faculty holding the doctorate. On the contrary, the proportion of PhD holders has risen enough in both employment categories (from 15% to 18% for part-timers and from 54% to 60% for full-timers) to offset the effect of casualization as well as that of disproportionate enrollment growth in the lower tiers of the system. Overall, the percentage of the United States' post-secondary faculty holding the doctorate actually rose during this decade, from 38% to 41%; and while we do not have separate statistics for English, the situation is encouraging in the humanities, where by 2003 PhD holders represented 64% of the faculty.[57] Moreover, if we look back to 1969, when the vast majority of faculty were full-time and teaching in 4-year institutions, what we find is not a golden age of consistently high standards of faculty qualification, but lower percentages of faculty holding the doctorate across the board.[58] The historical trend has been toward a better qualified faculty as well as one in which more and more professors, whether on the tenure track or not, are actively engaged in research. Though we can see this as employers offering less compensation for a given set of credentials and achievements, it is nevertheless clear that under the new managerialist regime, the American professoriate has undergone a process of smarting up rather than dumbing down.[59]

Credentials Fever

I am not suggesting that the global academy is safe from problems of declining qualifications and eroding faculty quality, or that the percentage of faculty with doctorates worldwide will approach the US level anytime in the near future. But when it comes to faculty credentials we are clearly dealing with a more complex and contradictory set of tendencies than the notion of dumbing-down suggests. The higher education boom is after all being driven in part by a kind of global credentials fever, a frenzy for degrees from which the educational apparatus itself is scarcely immune. Even the most egregious gutting of faculty hiring standards at the bottom of the tertiary system in countries like Mexico and China is partly a symptom of this fever for credentials, which has been superheating the market for qualified faculty at the top of the system, the tier of closely watched world rankings, and ever fiercer international competition. As Altbach points out, while only 9% of faculty in China hold doctoral degrees, the percentage at leading research universities is 70% – and that figure has been rising as the country pursues its ambition to put five universities into the world's top 100 and to become a major player in the scramble for international students, researchers, and recognitions.[60] The well-credentialed faculty at the high end of China's system are not paid nearly as well as their counterparts in Singapore, Japan, North America, or Europe, but their salaries are much closer to the world average than are those of China's low-end instructors. They make double what US faculty do when measured in relative terms (as a multiple of GDP per capita or of average household income), and despite nationally established pay scales, star faculty are reportedly making three or four times as much as ordinary senior professors, who are themselves making nearly three times as much as their entry-level colleagues.[61]

76

Fast-growing, ambitious national higher educational systems like China's are characterized by especially wide disparities, but they are the same disparities that characterize the entire global system. The globalization of higher education has fomented competition for increased access coupled with increased efficiency, which means lower and lower instructional costs, and lousier and lousier faculty jobs: this is the proverbial race-to-the-bottom effect of globalization. But it has also fomented competition for status at the high end, which means more and more universities and sponsoring states seeking to build and maintain "world-class" faculty – or at least to inch themselves upward a few rungs on the global rankings ladder, which now extends thousands deep into the regional and local higher education systems. This second effect of academic globalization is not simply an intensified competition for symbolic rewards. There are short-term and especially long-term material advantages to being an institution of choice for the most powerful and privileged (and to being the national home to such institutions). Today's CEOs may approve in principle the 100% contingent, 90% part-time, effectively deprofessorialized instructional corps at the predatory, for-profit University of Phoenix, but they will see to it that their own children attend Stanford or MIT, and this is the case for the advantaged classes throughout the world. If their national systems focus exclusively on efficiency and access, at the expense of ranking and reputation, then their children, too, will be sent to Stanford and MIT (or Toronto, Melbourne, Swiss Fed, San Paolo, Utrecht, or LSE).

There is thus an inherent limit in the process of degrading or dumbing down the professoriate. Even if all they did was to teach skills and thereby increase the "human capital" of the population, universities would need to employ trained and competent instructors. But that's not all they do or are expected to do by those who support and attend them. After all, most surveys suggest that university students really don't spend all that much time or energy on their studies; academic learning is a less vital part of what they do in college than we tend to realize. In the United Kingdom, full-time students during a typical week of term spend barely one quarter of their available hours on academic work, including the hours of attendance at lectures and labs.[62] A lot of what they do the rest of the time is social, mastering certain codes and strategies of interaction and installing themselves in durable networks of peers. Universities are expected to facilitate this social networking and to ensure that students make profitable connections and alliances, that they emerge from a degree program not just with more human capital but also with more social capital – both in the sense of interpersonal obligations or credits (friends and mentors they can "count on" professionally) and in the sense of know-how or feel for the social "game" of professional advancement. Similarly, while universities are taxed with the obligation to increase the educational capital of their graduates, this means not just to instill knowledge as such but also to confer a specific kind of cultural status (the status of the "educated"). The teaching of skills, especially the kind of skills that students can take away as portable learning strategies, does matter. But it matters as part of a more comprehensive agenda of "elevating," or conferring prestige, no less real a form of power than academic skills are. An Oxford degree is not more powerful than an Ohio State degree because the Oxford graduate can be counted on to have more fully mastered some specific kinds of task; it is more powerful because Oxford holds more status as an institution and thus confers more educational capital on its graduates, making them more attractive or worthy to prospective employers – and, not incidentally, to partners, spouses, and other kinds of associates, as well.[63]

Even the least distinguished state-run colleges and for-profit diploma mills have to be attentive to this question of their respectability or the perceived symbolic value of their transcripts. They, too, are forced (often by very specific financial incentives established by the state) to compete for greater status – higher ranking, wider recognition – as well as greater efficiency. While this sort of value is accumulated and maintained at the level of the institution, it derives in no small measure from the stature of the institution's faculty – in much the same way that the prestige of a cultural prize or award derives largely from the stature of its judges. In order to confer even a modicum of symbolic value on its graduates (the value equivalent of a minimally accredited, generic degree, with no name brand recognition or special good-will attaching to it), a university must employ faculty who are educated to at least the level of the degree being conferred on its graduates: to bachelor's level for teachers in bachelor's programs, master's level for teachers in master's programs, and doctoral level for teachers in doctoral programs. Where the educational capital of the faculty has been allowed to deteriorate below this basic threshold, such as has occurred at many of India's "affiliated colleges" over the last two decades, institutions face a catastrophic tipping point beyond which employers and even the public simply cease to credit their degrees. In the United States, the fast-growing private for-profit universities have had to be wary of this cusp of delegitimation; once leading the race to the bottom in terms of faculty credentials as well as faculty compensation – and even attempting to promote an academically impoverished faculty as better qualified, because they were more schooled in the "real world" than a properly credentialed one – they have reversed course in recent years, still lagging behind the nonprofit private and public universities but more rapidly increasing both the percentage of their faculty holding doctorates (or first professional degrees) and the salaries of their full-time faculty.[64] To rise above this baseline level of legitimacy and become truly competitive with the world's major institutions, a university has to seek out, and pay for, faculty who possess not just the minimum credentials but also an extra quantum of symbolic capital in their own right: high-status degrees and publications, distinguishing honors and accomplishments, a clear habit of scholarly productivity, and a strong reputation in their field.

What is going on with respect to faculty in most of the world's higher education systems is not simply a race to the bottom, as academic crisis narratives suggest, but a race also to this symbolic top, this upper tier of the global hierarchy. The challenge for the fastest growing, emergent systems, and the reason that overall standards with respect to faculty credentials are for the moment in a worrying state of decline, has to do with the temporality as well as the geography of academic prestige. Even with huge outlays of government money, symbolic capital cannot be accumulated overnight. It takes several academic generations for an existing national cohort of reputable (PhD-holding, research-publishing) scholars to produce a new cohort larger enough to produce in turn the still much larger cohort needed in order for the country to achieve even modest success in this race to the top. And in the meantime, or forever if your country fails in the process of accumulating educational capital, more and more of your best prepared and most promising students will take their degrees, and perhaps make their careers, abroad.

This process can be accelerated, but only a little, by recruiting faculty from abroad, making the more prestigious foreign faculty available domestically so that students needn't leave the country to study with them. Job markets in higher education remain more local and restricted than enrollments (which now include some 3.5 million degree seekers enrolled outside of their home countries, a number that is increasing by some 12% a year),[65] but there is a definite trend toward internationalization of the faculties, as well – particularly at the more competitive institutions. According to a recent survey, 70% of the world's 200 top-ranked universities had over the previous 2 years increased the proportion of their faculty drawn from foreign countries.[66] In rich countries such as Singapore and Saudi Arabia, where taking the quickest route into the upper echelons of the world ranking system is a matter of explicit national policy, foreigners can represent 40–50% of the senior faculty at some universities. The ratio is much lower in the United States and Europe, but growing rapidly, with the most esteemed institutions leading the way.[67] Education ministers and university administrators recognize that to be more "competitive" today means to be more "global" in this respect as in others; they have to seek and retain their research faculties in an increasingly borderless system boasting hundreds of would-be "world-class" institutions that are looking to do the same. One of the many advantages enjoyed by the established leaders in this institutional competition is that, on the whole, the international traffic in faculty follows the same itineraries as the traffic in students, that is, from less capitalized to more capitalized, from the developing to the developed world, from the Global South to the Global North, and from the aspiring nations to the dominant ones. Indeed, the traffic often involves the very same bodies, with for example a Chinese student doing her doctoral work in a British university, and then taking a faculty position in the United States or Singapore. For relatively unknown and unheralded universities to gain significant ground in this global scramble for the most desirable faculty, even the most desirable of their domestically produced faculty, is a huge challenge, and makes advancement in the rankings a slow and difficult process. Whichever rankings one consults – *US News*, *Times Higher Educational Supplement*, Shanghai Jao Tong, or the Cybometrics Lab's Webometrics Rankings – one rarely observes dramatic shifts of position from one year to the next, especially near the top. But it is in the nature of such a system to lodge the ambition for higher rankings, no less than that of cost efficiency, at the very heart of the higher educational agenda. For a particular university (e.g., the National University of Singapore) or a national university system (e.g., Malaysia's) to slide significantly downward on this global status ladder is enough to trigger all manner of alarum among the managers.

A global academic system that is driven in this way by competitive rankings – of individual degree programs, of universities, of local or state systems, of national and regional systems, and even of the academic ranking systems themselves – is in many respects abhorrent. That we now find universities ranked down to 6000th in the world (Virginia Highlands Community College, one rung below the Tianjin Urban Construction Institute) tells us just how far the new managerialism's narrowly and naïvely quantitative approach to matters of quality has now penetrated educational thinking. But it is this very form of thinking which, even as it imposes a regime of putative cost efficiency, also supports the value of the doctorate and assures growing demand for faculty who hold that degree.

How rapidly and how widely this global striving for recognition is affecting English studies are difficult to gauge. But if we survey the websites of leading universities in Central and Eastern Europe, and especially in Asia, we find many English departments that have been taking concrete steps to raise their research profiles: recruiting new faculty, founding new centers and institutes devoted to English-language literatures, developing new exchange relationships with English departments abroad, and so forth. These departments make a point of publicizing how many of their faculty hold the PhD, and a key piece of their institutional agenda has been to launch doctoral programs in English, or to significantly expand a program that already existed. At these kinds of institutions, the doctorate appears to be more and more central to the academic mission of English studies.

In Warsaw, to take just one example from post-Soviet Europe, we find ambitious and rapidly growing research programs in English at both the most established and the newest institutions. At the University of Warsaw, Poland's oldest and one of its most distinguished universities, enrollments have been soaring since the collapse of the Soviet Union, rising from fewer than 15,000 students in 1989 to more than 55,000 today, with the size of the faculty increasing nearly as fast. The English Department, which was quite small and produced only a handful of doctorates in the early 1990s, has undergone several rounds of expansion and restructuring over the past decade and a half, and is now the formidable English Institute, housing sections in English Linguistics (applied and theoretical), English Literature, American Literature, and the Cultures of Anglo-Saxon Countries. The faculty of these latter three sections alone consists of 33 professors, more than two thirds holding the PhD There are more than a hundred students in the PhD program, with half doing linguistics degrees and the other half specializing in literature or literary-cultural studies. The university also houses a separate American Studies Center, which dates back to the 1970s but has greatly expanded its faculty and launched a number of new postgraduate programs since the late 1990s. Currently employing more than 20 faculty, the center boasts interdisciplinary range but, as with American studies centers in the United States, the core of its curriculum lies in literature and history, with a third of the faculty holding higher degrees in English. Both the institute and the center sponsor many lectures and international conferences and have entered into cooperative arrangements with peer departments in the United States and throughout Europe.

If the University of Warsaw represents the state of English studies in the old, established quarters of Polish academe, the Warsaw School of Sciences and Humanities (SWPS) across the river is representative of the newer educational institutions that have emerged in the recent years of massification and Bologna-style restructuring. Officially licensed as a private institution, SWPS was founded in 1996 as an undergraduate college of social psychology but has rapidly expanded into other disciplines while building its enrollments to more than 10,000 and beginning to award higher degrees. We might imagine that this sort of new, private, social sciences-oriented college would have little time or space for English studies, especially at the higher level of research. But the school in fact launched a BA program in English studies within a few years of its founding, and in 2005, English became the first discipline after psychology to be offered at *Magister* (master's) level. As enrollments in the bachelor's and MA programs have climbed, the English faculty has grown to 22 members, arranged into an Institute of English Studies with three departments, focusing on EFL, linguistics, and English-language literature and culture. The last of these, specializing in literary study, is as large as the other two put together, and is the largest of all foreign language and literature departments at SWPS. All but one of the department's faculty hold the doctorate, and it appears likely that the school will begin offering its own PhD in English within a few years. The scale of its operation, as measured both by the events and lectures it sponsors and by its own research output, is much smaller than that of the Institute of English Studies at University of Warsaw. But taken together, these two Warsaw institutions, new and old, represent something quite different from the "dumbing down" of the English professoriate. They are part of a rising, vibrant community of Polish scholars doing high-level research and graduate teaching in English studies.

Similar communities of research faculty are emerging in Asian countries. Tsinghua University in Beijing, generally rated among China's top five and the top 100–200 in the world, is a case in point. Its Department of Foreign Languages and Literatures, which originally dates back to 1926 but was disbanded 40 years later at the start of the Cultural Revolution, was revived in modest form in 1983. For the next decade or so it was merely a service department stocked with instructional staff to teach the English language to students in other fields. But since the mid-1990s, much has changed. The department has greatly extended the range of its curricular offerings and faculty research to include "theoretical trends in modern western literature, modern British and American literature, Sino-western comparative literature, translation study and culture study." Its primary focus is now British, American, postcolonial, and world literature, and the department translates and publishes Chinese versions of *New Literary History* and *Critical Inquiry* as well as publishing its own literary journal, *Perspectives*. It has cohosted conferences with literature departments at Yale, Harvard, and Oxford. These changes have required a major effort to recruit "leading university professors . . . who lay particular emphasis on research." With that recruitment still ongoing, the faculty currently consists of about 20 full professors and 40 associate professors and lecturers, more than half of whom hold the doctorate. Within this faculty is a smaller Graduate Group comprising mostly PhD holders, which is now beginning to confer its own PhDs, having launched a doctoral program in English language and literature in 2003.

The PhDs emerging from fledgling programs like this one are in strong demand, being recruited not just by Tsinghua's internationally competitive peer institutions but also by smaller and more local colleges seeking to improve their standing in the national system. And while pay scales for beginning professors in China (on the order of $8,000 a year) are very low by US or European standards, and low even by the standards of Korea, Thailand, or Vietnam, they compare favorably to local salaries and are often buttressed by generous housing provisions and other perks and subsidies. They also offer more upside, that is, a steeper rate of salary increases over the course of a career, than in most of the wealthier countries. Since salary levels are set nationally by the Ministry of Education, compensation is far more adequate outside of the major coastal cities, and faculty in the provinces, where costs are low, live comfortably (albeit pining for the more vibrant academic scene on the coast). In expensive cities like Shanghai or Beijing, where housing prices have gone through the roof and campus housing for faculty is practically non-existent, recruitment has become a problem, especially recruitment of foreign faculty who cannot take advantage of the domestic support networks and who can just as readily do their teaching in Japan, Singapore, Vietnam, or other higher paying countries. A number of institutions in these cities have taken to offering salaries significantly higher than the Ministry stipulates, supplementing government funds with tuition revenue from foreign students. In fields such as management, professors at Peking University can make $75,000 or more.[68] And at the very top end, universities like Tsinghua have recently begun creating endowed chairs and term chairs on the American model of private patronage, seeking to attract "internationally renowned professors and scholars" with base pay starting at $100,000, a colossal income by local standards. The first of these chairs are presumably being used to furnish offices in business and science/technology departments, but if China continues on its current course, they will before too long begin to circulate among faculty in English, as well.[69]

The increasing demand for English doctorates and the resultant growth of English graduate programs in Asia are not restricted to China. We need to look past Japan, where a rising GER is being cancelled out by a shrinking college-age demographic,[70] as well as South Korea, which achieved essentially 100% enrollment in higher education several years ago and is now faced with a declining student population and a collapsing market for PhDs. Most of the other academic systems along the Pacific Rim, and especially the so-called Asian Miracle countries, have embarked on ambitious higher educational agendas that are driving institutions to seek more and better qualified faculty, with particularly strong demand for faculty who can teach Anglophone and especially US-oriented courses. In Taiwan, for example, there is a recognized shortage of doctorate-holding English instructors. The established Taiwanese universities are forced to compete for a very limited supply of candidates with small colleges that need to increase the proportion of PhDs on their faculty in order to upgrade to university status. Given that all these institutions, big and small, are chasing after a tiny domestic supply of new PhDs and a mere trickle of international applicants, qualified job candidates are in a good position. As in China, many institutions find themselves obliged to pay PhD holders more than the fixed pay grades set by the national government.[71] Though higher than in the People's Republic, those established salary levels still seem low from the vantage of Australia or North America. But, as in other Asian countries, salaries are augmented by various benefits and bonuses. A typical recent job listing (at National Tsinghua University) calls for applicants in American literature, Western drama, and linguistics at various levels from assistant through full professor and department chair. The set rate of salary for a beginning assistant professor is specified as $25,000, the state mandated level. But this excludes start-up expenses, housing allowance (which at many universities amounts to free housing), overtime pay for extra teaching or administrative work, substantial reward payments from the national government for article publications, and an annual bonus of at least 1.5 months' base salary after the first year of service – all of which are understood to be part of the "real" compensation figure, which is likely to be 50 percent or more above the base salary. Given the relatively low cost of living in most parts of the country, and the free medical care that is extended to all foreign workers in Taiwan, this is a good starting wage; in fact, according to cost-of-living calculators, it is more than an assistant professor would make in the United States. And full professors or department chairs in Taiwan make two to three times this amount.

It is not clear whether India will follow suit in this drive to recruit more and better qualified English faculty. Indeed, up until now India has shown little interest in competing in any kind of race to the top of the world's academic hierarchy. The expansion of the country's tertiary system, though still ongoing and as yet far below target enrollment levels, was already quite dramatic in the 1970s and 1980s. But broader access was achieved in those decades at the expense of quality; there was a general leveling of standards, with no particular effort made to sustain excellence of instruction or research at more elite institutions.[72] In the rush to accommodate more students, the system discounted especially the importance of the faculty, allowing classes to become unteachably large, and failing to provide adequate compensation, facilities, or support for research. The effect was to demoralize the professoriate and foster a cynical faculty culture in which one's academic title is mainly something to be put to profitable use off campus while the students on campus are thoroughly neglected.[73] These problems worsened in the 1990s as enrollments continued to soar while "regular" (i.e., full-time tenurable) faculty positions were effectively frozen. An enormous "nonregular" (i.e., contingent) instructional underclass emerged, poorly qualified and badly compensated, and apparently beyond the purview of state data collection and policy. At present, more than half the faculty in India's higher education system lack even a master's degree, let alone a PhD.[74]

India thus stands as something of an exception to the normal duplicity of effect in globalized higher education. There has been a downward pull on quality without the opposing clamber toward worldwide reputability and ranking among the leading research institutions.[75] It may be, however, that this unusual one-way course of massification has now gone about as far as possible and that counterpressures are beginning to emerge. Attention seems to be shifting back to the importance of regular full-time faculty, whose salaries have been raised substantially in recent years, and though still modest in absolute terms are now higher as a multiple of the national average income than even salaries in China, high enough that, according to one expert, "teachers can lead a comfortable middle-class life."[76] In addition, important changes have been made to hiring rules. Formerly, even the best of India's universities, the IITs (Indian Institutes of Technology, which, though oriented toward the engineering and information sciences, generally have respected graduate programs in English and other humanities fields), were prohibited from hiring foreign nationals to regular tenurable positions. These institutions had to be satisfied with whatever caliber of faculty the national system could produce, and leave vacant (or fill with temporary, adjunct instructors) many posts for which suitably trained research faculty simply weren't available. But the rule was changed in 2007 when the minister in charge of higher education, conceding a "dearth of qualified teachers in the field of higher education," approved international recruitment in order to jump-start the national infrastructure of academic research and doctoral training.[77] The IITs, along with a few other large national universities, have also been targeted in recent years for exceptional levels of financial support from the University Grants Council (UGC), with the aim of building and sustaining an elite tier in the academic system where research and doctoral-level teaching will be prioritized. In a somewhat broader initiative, the UCG has been expanding its Faculty Improvement Programme (FIP), which pays for existing college teachers to pursue MPhil or PhD degrees. The program covers tuition and living allowance for the degree candidate as well as the cost of hiring a temporary replacement instructor for up to 3 years of graduate study. English appears to be one of the disciplines that can best take advantage of these subsidies, with English departments enrolling the most graduate students on FIP grants.[78]

It remains to be seen whether these few modest steps are the start of a major shift toward the kind of large-scale training and recruitment of research-capable faculty that India's academic sector badly needs. At present, the world's second-largest Anglophone higher education system still stands as the most glaring example of how the global shift to mass enrollments has degraded professorial employment. But India may ultimately prove the unsustainability of this route and the inevitability of counter-pressures favoring stratification, with an elite sector of research universities pursuing a contrary agenda of global competitiveness. Given the scales involved, even a small fraction of India's English studies programs redirected toward the attainment of "world-class" stature would represent a significant addition to the sum of good jobs in the discipline: the kinds of faculty position where training, compensation, and support are pegged to adequate standards. While such jobs will in any case be greatly outnumbered by new contingent instructorships, the logic of global academe depends on their continued existence. A qualified professoriate in English, capable of training its own successors, remains, perhaps to the regret of the New Managers, a necessity.

Notes

1. On absolute versus relative numbers of tenure-stream faculty, see Alan Finder, "Decline of Tenure Track Raises Concerns," *New York Times* 20 November 2007. The American Association of University Professors (AAUP) tracks faculty salary increases versus the Consumer Price Index in its annual *Report on the Economic Status of the Profession*. According to the 2008–2009 report (Table 1), average inflation-adjusted salaries for all full-time faculty increased in 24 of the last 30 years, and for continuing faculty in 29 of the last 30 years. The widespread misperception among full-time faculty that their salaries have been declining seems to be a result of the rising differential between academic salaries and virtually all other professional salaries. To give just one example of this worsening "salary disadvantage" facing academics, legal professionals were making on average 43% more than university faculty in 1999 and had widened that gap to 62%, nearly half again as much, by 2003. But given that faculty salaries have risen relative to median income for the last 30 years (albeit very modestly), one should consider whether the problem to be rectified here is that of faculty salaries that are too low or, rather, that of other professional

salaries that have been allowed to rise too far from the median. See AAUP, *2008–09 Report on the Economic Status of the Profession*, http://www.aaup.org/NR/rdonlyres/AD0CDD44-CDCA-4FDD-825A-32FCC3746070/0/tab1.pdf. See also Martin J. Finkelstein and Jack H. Schuster, *The American Faculty* (Baltimore: Johns Hopkins University Press, 2006), 240–255.

2. As Philip G. Altbach explains, "The sort of legal or contractual guarantees [of continued academic employment] that exist in Europe and North America are not the norm elsewhere," but "many countries have 'de facto' tenure arrangements," and "most full-time academics spend their careers in a single institution." When I refer to tenure-stream faculty outside of the United States, I mean to include faculty subject to these "de facto" arrangements. Philip G. Altbach, "The Deterioration of the Academic Estate," in Altbach, ed., *The Changing Academic Workplace: Comparative Perspectives* (Chestnut Hill, MA: Boston College Center for International Higher Education, 2000), 19.

3. Faculty jobs in China initially take the form of 3-year contracts. A newly hired lecturer generally serves three such contracts, for a total apprentice period of 9 years, before becoming part of the permanent faculty. Associate professors normally serve out two contracts before being made permanent, and professors serve only one. In English studies, landing a first contract at a desirable (prestigious, coastal) university is becoming extremely difficult without a foreign (British, Australian, Canadian, or American) PhD. But once employed, job security is really not an issue.

4. The inability to think with statistics, and especially to distinguish between relative and absolute numbers, leads to much alarmist confusion among humanists. To take a recent example, in a 2010 *Chronicle of Higher Education* piece, Frank Donoghue cites "a fascinating study" of the "faculty hiring trends" in the British Commonwealth, which he believes "showed that between 1915 and 1995, the total number of faculty jobs in the humanities declined by 41 per cent, while the total number of faculty jobs in the social sciences increased by 222 percent." This is obviously nonsense. The total number of faculty in the humanities in 1915 was miniscule by today's standards; by 1995 that number had *grown* by thousands of percent. The study Donoghue cites did not track (absolute) changes in the "total number of faculty" but rather (rela-

tive) "changes in faculty composition." In 1915, the social sciences were only just beginning to emerge, and accounted for just a few percent of university faculty. As a percentage of the whole faculty, social scientists have become relatively more numerous, while the humanists and natural scientists have become less dominant. But in absolute terms, the humanities faculties, like the others, have experienced exponential growth, far outstripping both the population growth and the overall growth of the economies in the Commonwealth nations. See Frank Donoghue, "Can the Humanities Survive the 21st Century?" *The Chronicle Review* (5 September 2010): http://chronicle.com/article/Can-the-Humanities-Survive-the/124222/; and David John Frank and Jay Gabler, *Reconstructing the University: Worldwide Shifts in Academia in the 20th Century* (Stanford: Stanford University Press, 2006), 66, Figure 2.

5.   "Editorial Introduction," *Cambridge Quarterly* 34.3 (2005): 201.

6.   In 2006–2007, Princeton spent $140 million on faculty salaries, excluding all other instructional costs, such as stipends for graduate assistants, salaries for departmental staff, and overhead costs. With undergraduate enrollments of 4500 and graduate enrollments of 2000, faculty salaries thus cost more than $20,000 per student per year. The university's entire operating budget amounted to more than $150,000 per student. Such numbers are only possible at colossally well-endowed institutions. Even with the $100 million or so it collects in tuition each year, and the $200 million it receives in the form of research grants from government, corporate, and foundation sources, Princeton relies mainly on the income from its endowment, which (by the university's ultra-conservative accounting) generates $750 million in spendable income per year. Office of the Provost, Princeton University, *Report of the Priority Committee to the President: Recommendations Concerning the Operating Budget for 2006–07*, 13 January (Princeton, NJ: Princeton University, 2006), http://www.princeton.edu/%7Eprovost/pricomm/06-07/final-report.pdf.

7.   Annual expenditures per higher education student in selected countries, compiled from OECD data, are given in NCES, *Educational Indicators: An International Perspective, Expenditure for Education: 2003, Key Findings: France, Germany, Italy, Japan, United Kingdom, United States* (Washington, DC: NCES, 2003). Worldwide data on wealth distribution are analyzed in a 2008 working paper

by James Davies *et al.*, "The World Distribution of Household Wealth," February (London: World Institute for Development Economics Research of the United Nations University, 2008), http://www.wider.unu.edu/publications.

8. A widely publicized report from the Higher Education Research Institute (HERI) showed that not only elite private universities but also the top tier of state universities have been catering increasingly to the wealthy since 1985. Noting that at the most selective institutions, "more fathers of freshmen are doctors than are hourly workers, teachers, clergy members, farmers or members of the military – combined," the *New York Times* featured the HERI's findings on its front page, as part of a mounting body of evidence that our educational system is "reproducing social advantage instead of serving as an engine of mobility." David Leonhardt, "As Wealthy Fill Top Colleges, Concern Grows over Fairness," *New York Times*, 22 April 2004. More recently, *The Journal of Blacks in Higher Education* reported data from 1983 to 2006 showing that over this 23-year period, "eight of the 10 universities with the largest endowments have shown a *decline* in the percentage of low-income students in their student bodies." On average, such students now constitute fewer than 15% of Ivy League enrollments. See Henry Louis Gates Jr., "Ivy League Generosity Will Lure Affluent and Brightest Black Students Away from State Universities," *JBHE* (2008): http://www.jbhe.com/news_views/58_ivy_league_financial _aid.html. These and other studies confirm what left-wing sociologists of education – in France, Britain, the United States, and elsewhere – have long maintained: that the education system functions by and large as a means of euphemizing and thereby legitimating socioeconomic advantage. A major study in the mid-1990s by the National Opinion Research Center found that among US citizens, family income is the best single predictor of a child's eventual educational credentials – better than race, ethnicity, sex, or scores on achievement tests. See "Report Finds That Income Best Predicts Education," *New York Times*, 17 June 1996, A12.

9. A 2008 study by the Sutton Trust, a foundation whose aims include "democratizing admissions to leading schools," found that half of all entrants to Oxford and Cambridge came from just 200 "elite feeder schools" (8), 80% of which are private and nearly all of which are highly selective. From these schools, an average of 10%

of the university-bound graduates went to Oxbridge. The United Kingdom's other 3500 post-16 schools and colleges contributed barely one student each, or 1% of their university-bound graduates. The study found, moreover, that this systemic bias is trending toward greater elitism, with the very top schools increasing their share of Oxbridge admissions over time (11). Among the trust's broader findings was the fact that "there are many students from non-privileged backgrounds with high exam grades who do not end up at research-led universities. Basically put, a student in a state school is as likely to go on to a leading university as a student from the independent sector who gets two grades lower at A-level" (1). Sutton Trust, *University Admissions by Individual Schools*, February 2008, http://www.suttontrust.com/research/university-admissions-by-individual-schools/. Confirmation of these trends is found at the other end of the tertiary spectrum, where empirical studies of the New Universities suggest that the 1992 elevation of polytechnic schools to nominally equal footing with universities has merely replaced a strict hierarchical binary with a less transparent but equally effective system of "informal stratification." For an overview of the research, see Claire Sanders, "Analysis: Mixed Report for Class of '92," *Times Higher Education Supplement* 28 June 2002.

10. Pierre Bourdieu and Jean-Claude Passeron, *Reproduction in Education, Society, and Culture*, trans. Richard Nice (London: Sage, 1977).

11. Gender equity is the one great exception to this rule; in most countries, mass enrollment has vastly expanded women's share of educational capital, with a concomitant (though still substandard) rise in their expected lifetime income.

12. According to NCES figures in the *Digest of Education Statistics 2008*, http://nces.ed.gov/pubsearch/pubsinfo.asp?pubid=2009020. NCES has taken the figure of 8.8 million teachers in 2005 from the UNESCO Institute for Statistics.

13. NCES, *Digest of Education Statistics 2008*.

14. Geoffrey Channon, "Tailor-Made or Off-the-Peg: Virtual Courses in the Humanities," *Computers and the Humanities* 34 (2000): 255, quoted in Ellie Chambers and Marshall Gregory, *Teaching and Learning English Literature* (London: Sage, 2006), 7.

15. These figures are based on the UNESCO Global Digest 2006 and on the NCES report "Class Size and Ratio of Students to Teaching Staff, 2004," *Education Indicators: An International Perspective*

(http://www.nces.ed.gov/surveys/international). Figures for China are somewhat unreliable. While UNESCO puts the student–faculty ratio at 23.5, the Chinese Ministry of Education claims a much better ratio of 16.2. Even by the ministry's own reckoning, however, the ratio has risen 75% since 1994, when it was 9.2. See Uwe Brandenburg and Jiani Zhu, "Higher Education in China in Light of Massification and Demographic Change," Arbeitspapier No. 97, October (Gütersloh, Germany: Centrum für Hochschulentwicklung, 2007), 44, http://www.che.de/downloads/Higher_Education_in_ China_AP97.pdf. On India's failure to offer faculty salaries sufficient to fill vacant positions, see "India's Faculty Shortage Worsens, with 50% of Positions Vacant," news blog, *Chronicle of Higher Education* (6 October 2008): http://chronicle.com/article/ India-s-Faculty-Shortage/41747.

16. At China Central Radio and TV University, enrollment was reportedly 1.5 million students in 2003, with 1300 instructors overseeing 580 courses. There must obviously be many additional staff involved who are not counted among the "instructors." DeRen Chen and Wen Ying Guo, "Distance Learning in China," *Journal of Distance Education Technologies* 3 (October–December 2005): 1–5, esp. 2.

17. Even Philip G. Altbach, an undoubted authority in these matters, erroneously describes full-time faculty positions as though they are in a crisis of declining absolute numbers ("a decline in the number of full-time jobs" [137]) rather than of relative proportions. See his "The Deteriorating Guru: The Crisis of the Professoriate" and other of his essays collected in *International Higher Education: Reflections on Policy and Practice* (Chestnut Hill, MA: Boston College Center for International Higher Education, 2006).

18. The exceptions are countries where there have been no enrollment increases to offset rising student–teacher ratios. In Germany, for example, where enrollments have been flat since the 1990s, there have been reductions of academic staff at every rank and level. Between 1995 and 2005, more than 1400 professorships were eliminated, and some disciplines saw overall academic staff cuts of more than 20%. Linguistics and cultural studies, within which many English studies programs are housed, lost about 12%, nearly all of them tenured positions vacated by departures or retirements and then left unfilled. There are some signs, however, that Germany

has taken the downsizing of its professoriate too far, and that the government is reconsidering the approach. High student–faculty ratios have contributed to a sharp decline in the global status of Germany's once vaunted higher educational system. Even its best universities have fallen below 50th in recent world rankings. "Report: German Universities Lose Hundreds of Professors," *Deutsch Welle*, 21 August 2007, http://www.dw-world.de/dw/article/0,,2746123,00.html.

19. And, as discussed below, even the gold standard jobs are not what they used to be. In France, more than a third of the expansion of the (full-time, effectively tenured) professoriate has been achieved with teaching-only positions, which involve double the teaching load of traditional teaching-research appointments. These positions represented less than 10% of the professoriate in 1985 but nearly 20% in 1998. See Thierry Chevaillier, "French Academics: Between the Professions and the Civil Service," in Philip G. Altbach, ed., *The Changing Academic Workplace: Comparative Perspectives* (Chestnut Hill, MA: Boston College Center for International Higher Education, 2000), 93.

20. These statistics are derived from the National Center for Education Statistics, *Fall Staff in Postsecondary Institutions, 1995*, using the IPEDS Dataset Cutting Tool, US Department of Education National Center for Education Statistics, NCES 98303, 25 February 1998, http://nces.ed.gov/pubsearch/pubsinfo.asp?pubid=98303. As cited in ADE Ad Hoc Committee on Staffing, *Education in the Balance: A Report on the Academic Workforce in English*, report of the ADE Ad Hoc Committee on Staffing (New York: ADE, 2007), 3–5, esp. 22, Figure 3, http://www.mla.org/pdf/workforce_rpt02.pdf. For breakdown and analysis of this broad but uneven trend toward more part-time faculty, see the NCES report *Changes in Staff Distribution and Salaries of Full-Time Employees in Postsecondary Institutions: Fall 1993–2003* (Washington, DC: US Department of Education, 2006), esp. 16–17, Table 3.

21. Data for Figure 2.3 taken from NCES, *Digest of Education Statistics 2009*, Table 249: "Number of Instructional Faculty in Degree-Granting Institutions, by Employment Status, Sex, Control, and Type of Institution: Selected Years, Fall 1970 through Fall 2007." The smoother curve for the number of faculty tenured or on tenure track in Figure 2.3 reflects the fewer available data points

in that category, which were derived from the US Department of Education *Fall Staff Surveys* (*2005 Fall Staff Survey*, http://nces. ed.gov/IPEDS) by the AAUP for its *Contingent Faculty Index* 2006. Figure 1 in the latter document shows the percentage of faculty tenured or on tenure track in 1975 (57%), 1989 (47%), and 2003 (35.1%). Despite the rapid decline in these percentages, absolute growth has been strong enough to maintain a slightly positive slope to the curve.

22. Philip G. Altbach, "It's the Faculty, Stupid! The Centrality of the Academic Profession," *International Higher Education* 55 (Spring 2009): 15–17. Altbach points out that Brazil is an exception. Indeed, at Brazil's leading universities, such as Sao Paulo, the 80:20 ratio is completely reversed, with more than 80% of the faculty employed full-time (and, to anticipate the discussion below, more than 90% holding the doctorate).

23. Li Zhifeng *et al.*, "Institutional View of Part-Time Faculty Management in Higher Education Institutes in China," *Frontiers of Education in China* 2.2 (2007): 287, Table 1.

24. Peter Schmidt, "Use of Part-Time Faculty Tied to Lower Student Success," *Chronicle of Higher Education* 14 November 2008.

25. For an excellent overview of the different forms of contract and expectations of security in academic employment around the world, see Altbach, "The Deterioration of the Academic Estate," 15–19.

26. Altbach, "Deterioration of the Academic Estate," 18.

27. HESA, *Summary of Academic Staff (Excluding Atypical) in All UK Institutions 2007/08*, http://data.gov.uk/dataset/hesa-summary-of-academic-staff-excluding-a-typical-in-all-uk-institutions.

28. The absolute number of tenure-stream (or de facto equivalent) faculty has remained constant in the United States and has risen sharply in some of the fastest growing national educational systems. But in every country I have examined, this group represents a smaller and smaller fraction of the total instructional workforce.

29. Schmidt, "Use of Part-Time Faculty."

30. In describing these new conditions of academic labor as effects of late-capitalist managerialism, I don't mean to overstate the parallels between the nonprofit research university and the corporation. Andrew Ross has argued that the glaring inefficiencies and hyper-bureaucratization of the universities suggest a political rather than

a corporate model. The latter model has for two decades stipulated "a drastic thinning-out of middle-management ranks," while higher education has during that period seen an "amassing of administrative ranks" more reminiscent of Washington or the United Nations than of Wall Street. My view, as I try to suggest in regard to the British case, is that the emerging global model of the research university is born of a forced convergence between the two other paradigms: political bureaucratization joined to corporate-style accounting and rationales. See Andrew Ross, "The Corporate Analogy Unravels," *The Chronicle Review* 22 October 2010: B18.

31. In the United States, over the decade 1993 to 2003, the only academic employee category for which salary increases outpaced the rise in average household income was "executive, administrative, and managerial." *NCES, Changes in Staff Distribution and Salaries of Full-Time Employees in Postsecondary Institutions: Fall 1993–2003* (Washington, DC: US Department of Education, 2006), xiv.

32. The basic trend was already observable in the United States in the 1980s. The Higher Education General Information Survey reported that the share of operating budget spent on instruction at US colleges and universities was 4 percent lower in 1985 than in 1975, while the share spent on administration was 13 percent higher (John Freeman, "Why College Costs Are Rising," *The Freeman* 38.11 [November 1988]: http://www.thefreemanonline.org/columns/why-college-costs-are-rising/). Since then, academic expenses have continued to shrink in proportion to the total budget at about this same rate, while administrative expenses have enlarged their share even faster. For an array of charts and graphs illustrating this tendency, see the website of the Center for College Affordability and Productivity at http://www.centerforcollegeaffordability.org. For a specific example, consider Cornell, where between 1995 and 2005, the share of the operating budget devoted to academic programs was trimmed from 73% to 71% while the share devoted to "administrative and support costs" was expanded by more than half, from 7.8% to 12.3%. Suzy Gustafson, "As University Tuition Grows, Administrative Costs Do, Too," *The Cornell Daily Sun*, 10 October 2007.

33. A good brief history of these developments is Robert Phillips, "Education, the State, and the Politics of Reform: The Historical

Context, 1976–2001," in John Furlong and Robert Phillips, eds., *Education, Reform, and the State* (London: Routledge, 2001), 12–28, esp. 20–24. For a large-scale empirical study of the effects of this "New Managerialism" in Britain's higher education system, see Rosemary Deem, "Managing Contemporary UK Universities – Manager-Academics and New Managerialism," *Academic Leadership: The Online Journal* 1.3 (12 February 2007): 3–10.

34. "Free Lecturers from the Never-Ending Burden of Administration, Says Union," *Western Mail* (Cardiff) 5 June 2008.

35. As of 2004. From UNESCO, *UNESCO Digest 2006*, http://www.uis.unesco.org/Library/Documents/ged06-en.pdf, 134, Table 10: "International Flows of Mobile Students at the Tertiary Level / 2004."

36. Joshua Ka-Ho Mok and Anthony R. Welch, "Economic Rationalism, Managerialism and Structural Reform in Education," in Ka-Ho Mok and David Kin-Keung Chan, eds., *Globalization and Education: The Quest for Quality Education in Hong Kong* (Hong Kong: Hong Kong University Press, 2002), 33–34.

37. According to the ADE report *Education in the Balance*, 46, Table 2, 3100 full-time tenure-stream positions were lost during the 12-year span from 1993 to 2004, and 1400 part-time or nontenurable positions created.

38. MLA Office of Research, *Report on the MLA Job Information List, 2009–10*, September (New York: Modern Language Association, 2010), http://www.mla.org/pdf/sept_rpt_jil0910.pdf.

39. "Report of the ADE Ad Hoc Committee on Changes in the Structure and Financing of Higher Education," *ADE Bulletin* 137 (Spring 2005): http://www.ade.org/reports/ADEadhoc_Structure&finance.htm.

40. Marc Bousquet, "The Rhetoric of 'Job Market' and the Reality of the Academic Labor System," *College English* 66 (2003): 207–228.

41. See Marc Bousquet, *How the University Works: Higher Education and the Low-Wage Nation* (New York: New York University Press, 2008), 15–21; also Frank Donahue, *The Last Professors: The Corporate University and the Fate of the Humanities* (New York: Fordham University Press, 2008) 33–38. The derogatory characterization of academic "job market" rhetoric in these critiques is often persuasive. But neither Bousquet nor Donahue acknowledges that there

really is a demand, a perceived need on the part of the United States' corporate university employers, for about 500 new PhDs in English every year. Nor do they explain why tenured faculty in English should be complicit in the production of more than twice that number, year after year. Donahue need only look at his curriculum vita to see that his own tenure track employment (first tenurable job in 1986, second in 1989) came precisely in that handful of years when PhD production was reduced to the suppressed demand level of the managerialist era.

42. This it seems to me is the potential quietist implication of Bousquet's properly ferocious critique of the rhetoric of the "job market": the term, he argues, is a euphemism for a ruthlessly exploitative system within which the "supply" of noncontingent academic jobs is a fiction. Any effort to undersupply this (false) market will be quickly and eagerly countered by even higher rates of casualization. I am in agreement with much of the analysis in Bousquet's book, but what might be called the "boutique" fraction of the professoriate appears to be a fairly stable reality that might be used to put a floor under the collapsing terms of academic labor and even to gain some purchase for renegotiating those terms. As I argue below, the evidence of the late 1980s suggests that there are at least some advantages to limiting the scale of our graduate programs. In any case, no serious collective effort to do so has been mounted.

43. "A Few Good Professors: US Business Schools Suffer a Dearth of Doctorates," Knowledge@W.P.Carey (W.P. Carey School, University of Arizona) 6 June 2007, http://knowledge.wpcarey.asu.edu/article.cfm?articleid=1426.

44. Doctoral statistics are taken from American Academy of Arts & Sciences, *Humanities Indicators, Second Edition* (2010), Part II: Undergraduate and Graduate Education in the Humanities, Figure II-18c: "Doctoral Degree Completions in English Language and Literature (Absolute Numbers and as a Percentage of all Doctorates, 1966-2009)," and the accompanying spreadsheet, http://www.humanitiesindicators.org/content/hrcoII.aspx. Data compiled from US Department of Education, Institute of Education Sciences, National Center for Education Statistics, Integrated Postsecondary Data System, and accessed by the American Academy of Arts & Sciences via the National Science Foundation's online integrated science and engineering resources data system, WebCASPAR.

45. The 80% figure is taken from Nerad and Cerny's discussion of the results for English graduates of the University of California, Berkeley's excellent *PhD's – Ten Years Later* study of 1999. Unfortunately, the subjects of this study took their degrees between 1982 and 1985; there are no comparable data from the relatively good years of 1987–1990 or from more recent years. Merasi Nerad and Joseph Cerny, "From Rumors to Facts: Career Outcomes of English PhDs – Results from the *PhD's – Ten Years Later* Study," *Communicator* 32 (Fall 1999): 4.

46. That first tenurable position is all the more important because the drive to casualize faculty has not reduced the odds of a tenure-track job leading to a tenured one. According to Table 5 in the introduction to the invaluable *2007–2008 Humanities Departmental Survey,* http://www.humanitiesindicators.org/resources/survey. aspx, about 90% of English faculty who come up for tenure are granted it. Even allowing for faculty who leave before coming up, nearly three quarters of those who are on the tenure track end up tenured.

47. For job placement statistics, see *Placement Outcomes for Modern Language PhDs: Findings from the MLA's 2003–04 Survey of PhD Placement,* http://www.ade.org/reports, 80, Figure 1. For analysis of these findings in the context of the changing economics of American higher education, see the "Report of the ADE Ad Hoc Committee on Changes in the Structure and Financing of Higher Education."

48. William G. Bowen and Julie Ann Sosa, *Prospects for Faculty in the Arts and Sciences: A Study of Factors Affecting Demand and Supply, 1987–2012* (Princeton, NJ: Princeton University Press, 1989).

49. American Academy of Arts and Sciences, *Humanities Indicators.* As a percentage of all doctoral degrees, PhDs in English have fallen sharply over the last decade, from over 3% down to about 2%. But in absolute numbers there has been little change since 2001.

50. For data on attrition and completion, see the reports and updates published by the Council of Graduate Studies as part of their ongoing PhD Completion Study, at http://www.phdcompletion. org/quantitative. While it is true that completion rates in English seem low (about 50% after 10 years) and attrition rates high (about 26% after 10 years), these are better percentages than in other fields

of the humanities and on par with many of the social, mathematical, and physical sciences.

51. "Education in the Balance," Figure 17b and 17d.
52. John Guillory, "Preprofessionalism: What Graduate Students Want," *ADE Bulletin* 113 (Spring 1996): 4–8.
53. Altbach, "It's the Faculty, Stupid!"
54. Altbach, "It's the Faculty, Stupid!"
55. David W. Breneman and Susan C. Nelson, *Financing Community Colleges: An Economic Perspective*, Studies in Education Series (Washington DC: Brookings Institution Press, 1981), 1.
56. *Digest of Education Statistics 2007*, Table 242.
57. *Digest of Education Statistics 2007*, Tables 242 and 244.
58. A good overview of the data is provided in Finkelstein and Schuster, *The American Faculty*, Appendix Table A-6.1: "Full-Time Faculty Holding Doctorate, 1969–1998," 513.
59. The percentage of full-time faculty reporting no publications over their entire career has declined from 33% in 1969 to 21% in 1998; those reporting no publications over the most recent 2 years have declined from 50% to 33%. Finkelstein and Schuster, Appendix Table A-4.9: "Research and Publication Activity as Reported by Full-Time Faculty, 1969-1998," 474. Unfortunately, while these data include non-tenure-track faculty, they omit part-time faculty. It seems to me likely, however, that part-time faculty are following the same trendlines, given that they are now twice as likely as they were in 1969 to hold research degrees, and are subject to far more intense publication pressure.
60. Originally, China targeted 2010 to achieve the goal of five universities in the world's top 100. But that has proved over-ambitious; as of 2011, only Tsinghua and Peking Universities in Beijing appear in the top 100 on any of the major rankings lists, and some lists rank them much lower. With so many of the world's national systems and individual institutions chasing higher rankings, the cost of admission to the top-100 club is continually rising.
61. Laura E. Rumbley, Ivan F. Pacheco, and Philip G. Altbach, *International Comparison of Academic Salaries: An Exploratory Study* (Boston: Boston College Center for International Higher Education, 2008), 20–25, 37–38.
62. Philip Stevens and Martin Weale, "Lazy Students? A Study of Student Time Use," National Institute of Economic and Social

Research working paper, rev. 10 May 2004, http://www.niesr.
ac.uk/pubs/dps/Dp233.pdf.

63. "Of course," as Ahwa Ong points out in her discussion of how
foreign cultural capital converts into local power and prestige,
"there are local configurations, so among some aristocratic
European circles, flaunting one's American business degree may be
considered petit bourgeois rather than haute culture." Ong, *Flexible
Citizenship: The Cultural Logics of Transnationalism* (Durham, NC:
Duke University Press, 2005), 90.

64. Garry Boulard, "Report Finds Faculty Pay Up – Barely," *Diverse:
Issues in Higher Education* 24 February 2005. The argument in favor
of a nontraditional faculty whose credentials consist of "practical
experience" rather than academic attainments has long been in play
at local technical colleges and other vocational institutions, including the pre-1992 polytechnics in Britain. For-profit universities
that have lately promoted this view in the United States, such as the
University of Phoenix, have been making the case not just for
under-credentialing but also for contingency. Their claim is that
part-time teacher-practitioners, being less academic and more
immersed in the world of their "full-time careers," can provide
students with the right educational balance of "theory and practice." See http://www.phoenix.edu/faculty/our_faculty.html.

65. As given in a BBC advance report on the UNESCO Institute for
Statistics 2011 data. See Sean Coughlan, "Record Numbers of
International Students," *BBC News* (9 March 2011).

66. Cited by Mike Baker, "China's Bid for World Domination," *BBC
News*, 17 November 2007, http://news.bbc.co.uk/2/hi/uk_news/
education/7098561.stm.

67. According to the National Center for Educational Statistics, "non-
resident aliens" as a percentage of all full-time instructors at
degree-granting institutions in the United States tripled between
1993 and 2003. Kenneth Foote *et al.*, "Foreign-Born Scholars in
US Universities: Issues, Concerns, and Strategies," *Journal of
Geography in Higher Education* 32 (May 2008): 167–178, esp. 169.

68. According to Weiying Zhang, assistant president of Peking
University, full professors in the University's Gwanghua School of
Management were already earning $60,000 in 2006. Pallavi Aiyar,
"China Hunts Abroad for Academic Talent," *Asia Times* (18

February 2006), China Business sec., online ed., http://www. atimes.com/China_Business.

69. As at most institutions, these chairs are available to all schools and departments at Tsinghua on a competitive basis. See Tsinghua University, "Charter for Chair Professorship Funds," http://www. tsinghua.edu/eng/employment.jsp.

70. Japan is not a country in which English literary study ever claimed a significant share of the curriculum. Foreign literature departments in general tend to be quite small, and English studies is mostly given over to EFL. And from the standpoint of foreign nationals, the country's professoriate is a relatively closed shop. Nevertheless, some of the same general hiring patterns obtain here as elsewhere: more part-time and contingent faculty at the low end, especially in private colleges and local public universities, but also more competition for highly qualified faculty with research degrees at the high end. Research is a fundamental expectation in the public sector and in the more ambitious private institutions, even for those whose teaching consists largely of foreign language courses. All full-time faculty in the national universities, including EFL instructors, are expected to publish articles, author textbooks, participate in professional organizations, and undertake conference travel (paid for by the universities). Charles Jannuzi, a professor at Fukui University, has written a number of good articles and opinion pieces about teaching English in the Japanese higher education system; these are available on his blog "Japan Higher Education Outlook" (JHEO), http://japanheo.blogspot. com.

71. There is much information about hidden salary and perks in the "University Teaching" section of Michael Turton's website *Teaching English in Taiwan*, http://www.michaelturton.com/Taiwan/teach_ index.html#college.

72. Philip Altbach, "A World-Class Country without World-Class Higher Education: India's 21st-Century Dilemma," *International Higher Education* 40 (Summer 2005): 18–20. For a more neutral overview, see the World Bank, "Country Summary of Higher Education" for India, http://siteresources.worldbank.org/ EDUCATION/Resources/278200-1121703274255/1439264- 1193249163062/India_CountrySummary.pdf.

73. A gloomy assessment of the Indian professoriate is N. Jayaram, "The Fall of the Guru: The Decline of the Academic Profession in India," in Philip G. Altbach, ed., *The Decline of the Guru: The Academic Profession in Developing and Middle-Income Countries* (Chestnut Hill, MA: Boston College Center for International Higher Education, 2002), 207–239.
74. Jason Overdorf, "When More Is Worse (Special Report: The Education Race)," *Newsweek* 25 August 2008.
75. The Indian School of Business in Hyderabad, which has climbed into the top 15 in rankings of the world's MBA programs, might be considered an exception – though it is of course a professional school rather than a research university as such.
76. Jayaram, "Fall of the Guru," 222.
77. Shailaja Neelakantan, "Top Universities in India Will Look Abroad for Faculty Members," *Chronicle of Higher Education* 27 August 2007.
78. Admittedly, the program has thus far been rather ineffectual; among other things, the very shortage of qualified faculty that FIP is meant to help alleviate means that replacement instructors are hard to come by. This in turn discourages college administrators from approving their faculty's participation.

Part III

The Future of the English Curriculum

Literary Studies in Its Global Aspect

The End of the Discipline as We Know It

The foregoing part of this book was not intended to deny the problems that faculty in English are confronting as the world's university system continues on its trajectory of massification. To be an English professor today – if one can even land the job – is to face increasing instructional and administrative workloads and/or rising expectations of scholarly production, combined with infinitesimal salary raises and, in many countries, reduced security and status of employment. But this is a version of what is happening not only to other faculty in other disciplines but also to practically all workers at all levels save that of upper management. As educated professionals, holders of higher degrees, we might wish to be included in that top echelon, insulated from the brutalities of labor casualization and income polarization. But a mass higher education system is too large and too labor intensive to comprise an elite instructional force; however disadvantaged we may be relative to the other professions, university faculty cannot reasonably aspire beyond middle-class status.[1]

The problem is that, throughout the developed and some parts of the developing world, the middle class is being destroyed by the

The Global Future of English Studies, First Edition. James F. English.
© 2012 John Wiley & Sons, Ltd. Published 2012 by John Wiley & Sons, Ltd.

wealthy, who have contrived to install national and international systems of governance that essentially function as economic check valves, permitting speculative profit to flow freely through to their private accounts while the massive cyclical losses are backed up in the form of public debt and impoverishment. The United States built the most lavishly furnished and capable university system in the world through a 30-year period (1950 through 1980) when the total share of GDP devoted to higher education was about the same as that devoted to the financial industry (3%). Today, the country's hedge funds, investment banks, and other financial institutions consume more than twice as much as its higher educational sector – more, in fact, than the entire education system combined, private as well as public, from pre-school through the PhD.[2] The financial sector has pocketed 40% of all corporate profits for the last decade while corporate profit has come to represent an unprecedented share of our economic growth. A recent study shows that, more than 2 years into the recovery from the 2007–2009 recession, corporate profit had captured 88% of the growth in national income, as against less than 1% by aggregate wages and salaries.[3] These numbers describe a society of grotesquely misallocated resources, sustained by an unconscionable tax code, a gutted regulatory regime, and an election-financing system that amounts to institutionalized corruption. And while the United States is a fairly extreme case, the tilting of the economic tables away from the public and the many toward the private and the few is clearly a global phenomenon: witness Spain, Greece, Russia, the United Kingdom, and so on. We need to temper the rhetoric of disciplinary crisis insofar as it partakes of exceptionalism and special pleading. There is indeed a crisis, and we are experiencing it in our places of work, but it is not specifically *our* crisis, an English professors' crisis. Nor will it be in any way ameliorated by more widespread study of Shakespeare. In relative terms, and in a global perspective, the higher study of English literature has shown itself to be a surprisingly resilient and durable field of educational practice; its salvation is not the issue.

Few of us are entirely willing to accept this view of things. Morale among the professoriate appears, anecdotally at least, to be at an all-time low. Even the fact of our discipline's continuing and rapid global expansion, as detailed in Part I, does not allay the fears of its erosion and imminent collapse. For many of us, the growth of enrollments in and of itself is not reassuring. There remains a concern that what is expanding is not really the discipline of English, that the discipline as we (in the United Kingdom or North America) ordinarily understand it *is* in fact shrinking, being replaced by programs that, though sometimes bearing the same name or taught by the same faculty, are actually quite different: programs in ESL, remedial writing, business English, Anglophone area studies, rhetoric and composition, practical communication, applied linguistics, media arts, and so on. We respond with alarm to this seeming eclipse of *real* English studies: the novel, the sonnet, or even the classic film being replaced in the English department's curriculum by the lab report, the business memo, or the executive summary; and literary scholars being hired to teach courses like English for Scientists or Basics of Organizational Communication instead of seminars on Dickens or Faulkner.

The anxieties and resentments involved here are memorably evoked in the opening pages of J.M. Coetzee's novel *Disgrace*. Cape Town University College, where Coetzee's protagonist, David Lurie, was formerly a professor of English literature, has abolished its department of classics and modern languages and rebadged itself Cape Technical University. In this now "emasculated institution of learning" (more devoted, as he sees it, to caregiving or social work than to the advancement of knowledge), Lurie is deployed as an adjunct professor of communications, his teaching for the most part consisting of just two courses: "Communications 101, 'Communication Skills,' and Communications 201, 'Advanced Communication Skills'" (3). He is permitted one special-field course a year, on Romantic poetry, but these literary seminars, kept running only for the sake of faculty "morale," appear neither to boost his spirits nor to generate much excitement among the handful of bemused students who sign on for them (4).

The novel gives us to believe that these are the straitened circumstances of English literary studies in the wake of what Lurie calls "the great rationalization": the opening of the doors of South Africa's higher education system to the country's black majority, and the concomitant retooling of the old white-elite curriculum to better serve the needs of this larger and less advantaged population. And indeed, since 1993 the country's higher educational enrollments have grown by more than 75%,[4] and much of that growth is attributable to the rising number of black students, which increased from a small fraction of the total in the early 1990s to a majority by the end of the decade and nearly two thirds in 2010.[5] But though it is rendered here in terms of the economic and political realities specific to post-Apartheid South Africa, the scenario resonates for Coetzee's global readership because it is a global commonplace that democratization and massification of the post-secondary system mean the contraction and death of literary study, that ours is a discipline too rarified to survive the more pragmatic agendas of mass higher education. David Lurie is just one of the world's many literature professors who perceive themselves as anachronistic, "burdened with upbringings inappropriate to the tasks they are set to perform" (4). His professional outlook is not so different from that of William Deresiewicz at Yale, lamenting students' supposed abandonment of English for the sake of more "practical" majors.

But like Deresiewicz's, Coetzee's representation of academe is less realism than dystopian projection. The author was himself a professor of English literature at the University of Cape Town through the final decades of Apartheid governance and the first decade of democracy, and he witnessed there no very dramatic reorganization of the English department, let alone any grand scheme to replace literary study with communications. Even today, English majors at UCT – of whom there are considerably more than there were in 1993 – must follow a rigorously high-literary curriculum. First-year students are required to enroll in English Literary Studies I (consisting of *Antony and Cleopatra*, *Pride and Prejudice*, *Great Expectations*, *Heart of Darkness*, and the *Norton*

Anthology of Poetry), followed by English Literary Studies II (*Passage to India*, *Death of a Salesman*, plus Hanif Kureishi, Zakes Mda, and more poetry from the *Norton*).[6] In the second year, students normally take one course in South African literature (which involves more Mda, some Fugard, and quite a lot of Coetzee) and one or both surveys of English literature (a Renaissance survey called Shakespeare and Company, featuring *Canterbury Tales*, *Hamlet*, *Paradise Lost*, and *Oronooko*; and an eighteenth- and nineteenth-century survey called Romance to Realism, featuring *Robinson Crusoe*, *Frankenstein*, *Jane Eyre*, and *The Scarlet Letter*). Along with these lecture classes, students must select corresponding seminars on such themes as Shakespeare's Tragedies or Global Shakespeare in the fall and Tristram Shandy or The Poetry of John Keats in the spring. The core courses in the third year focus on Modernism (Woolf, Joyce, Conrad, Faulkner, and Eliot) and Postmodernism (Nabokov, Ellison, Pynchon, and again Coetzee). There are, as we would expect, a substantial range of electives in African literature. But by and large, the curriculum is centered on a traditional (male) British and, to a lesser degree, American literary canon. This is true as well at other, less prestigious research universities in the region, such as the University of the Western Cape, whose English department inclines somewhat more toward electives in film and media but requires all majors to do substantial coursework in myth and literature (Ovid, Homer, Milton, and Shelley's *Frankenstein*), the Renaissance (Shakespeare, More, Machiavelli, and Marlowe), nineteenth-century literature (key texts include *Wuthering Heights*, *Tale of Two Cities*, and *Story of an African Farm*), and modernism (Conrad, Forster, Lawrence, and Shaw). No sign here of Communications 101. Remedial classes in "academic literacy" are taught entirely outside the English Department, under the nondepartmental auspices of the Language Development Group and the Writing Centre. Courses in spoken communication, business writing, and other areas of applied or vocational English are likewise handled by a separate instructional workforce, in a para-academic unit called Professional Communication Studies and Services. The existence of these courses no more imperils the faculty in English than it does the faculty in molecular biology. The students in the English department in fact face more stringent requirements in the established canon and traditional critical methods than are imposed on most majors in the United States or the United Kingdom.

As for a grand shift toward more technical or vocational education, this is a complicated matter. Yes, in most national debates over higher education there is great emphasis on the workplace readiness of college graduates and the match between the skills they acquire as students and the skills employers are looking for. But this does not necessarily mean that such emphasis is greater today than it used to be, much less that it is more determining of the curricular paths students actually take through college. Recall that in the largest and most advanced higher education systems the fastest growing sector has for some time been the humanities and performing arts. There has certainly been no diminishment of the perennial complaining from employers that students are choosing the "wrong" disciplines and failing to acquire the requisite job skills. And indeed employers have been providing more remedial education for their college-educated workers than ever before.[7] It is simply not clear that the massification of the baccalaureate program has meant its vocationalization. The dominant tendency in South Africa, as in the United States, the United Kingdom, China, and elsewhere, has been just the opposite of what Coetzee depicts: not comprehensive universities shutting down liberal arts departments in order to become more like polytechnics (a rare phenomenon), but technical colleges extending and expanding their curricula in order to become more like comprehensive universities. It remains a matter of debate whether we should commend this tendency as providing less privileged students with access to a full-blown liberal arts education, or rather condemn it as shifting resources into areas unsuited to both the educational preparation and the vocational needs of those students (and thereby driving up their need for vocational education *after* college).[8] But it is a major global trend, evident even in Australia, where an enduring national tilt toward vocationalism and preprofessionalism, having survived the wholesale integration of technical colleges into the national university system two decades ago, is now being further challenged by the so-called Melbourne Model of the liberal arts baccalaureate.[9] Likewise in India, where higher education has long been focused obsessively on engineering, there is a discernible retreat from pure vocationalism. The Indian Institutes of Technology (IITs) have begun moving toward the model of tech-oriented US universities where strong offerings in the liberal arts complement an overall emphasis on science and technology. A report by the Committee to Advise on Renovation and Rejuvenation of Higher Education in India concluded that the ITTs, as well as the Institutes of Management, must "strive to be models of all-round excellence, like the famous Massachusetts Institute of Technology or CalTech in the US":[10]

> This requires rethinking to prevent isolation of the study of engineering and management from other knowledge areas. This realization is reflected in the initiatives of some of the IITs that aim to introduce humanities and other disciplines and expand their scope. These initiatives strengthen our argument that they need to broaden their curriculum framework and assume the functions of full-fledged universities without losing their unique character. We can then look forward to the day when IITs and IIMs would be producing scholars in literature, linguistics and politics along with engineering and management wizards. (15)

Of course, there are in South Africa as all over the world many technological institutions that are geared mainly to vocational training. In Cape Town, there is the Cape Peninsula University of Technology (CPUT), running a curriculum devoid of any courses in classical or modern literatures. But CPUT emerged not from the rationalization of a more comprehensive or liberal college but from a merger of Cape Technical College with Peninsula Technical College, both of which have always been strictly oriented toward science and technology. Not only has there been no loss to literary studies in the formation of this larger, post-merger university, but we may anticipate that the curriculum there will over time extend itself toward the zones of communications and ultimately even arts and letters – as has happened, for example, at Durban University of Technology, which was similarly created from the merger of two "technikons," and which now houses within its expanded Faculty of Arts a Department of Media, Language and Communication offering degree tracks in both English and translation studies.[11]

Coetzee's ironies are complex, especially with regard to his literary intellectual figures (David Lurie, Elizabeth Costello, Señor C—, and the "He" of the memoirs). The valences of sympathy, satire, and critique in *Disgrace* are notoriously difficult to pin down. But if the novel captures an important truth about higher education and English studies in the era of globalization, it is a psychological rather than an institutional truth, a truth about fears and regrets that have come to characterize the literary professoriate rather than about who is actually teaching and studying what where. Whatever the intention, satiric or otherwise, with his embittered protagonist and dystopian academic setting, Coetzee gives expression to an altogether orthodox anxiety: that the once noble discipline of English, though surviving after a fashion, has lost its rigor, its integrity, its intellectual force – and even, for some, its manliness: that it has become a lowly service wing of the global university system, providing basic skills training in "English-as-literacy" to students whose academic and life ambitions lie ever further from the core mission of literary study.[12]

I will attempt in this third part of the book to provide an alternative, less familiar picture of the profession based on research into the actual courses, requirements, and curricular tendencies in English departments around the world. It will show that the discipline has to a considerable extent preserved its traditional aims and emphases through the period of higher education's global massification and the rise of English as a world language. We will see that the curriculum in English studies remains anchored in a literary canon, and that while there are some trends drawing it away from that traditional mooring, the discipline is not devolving into remedial language learning or vocationally oriented media studies.

While this view of the matter cannot hope to compete for sheer visceral impact with the horrifying visions of ruin on offer elsewhere, it does have the advantage of being – within its admittedly limited compass – empirically true.

Language versus Literature

In observing that Coetzee's own former department, the English Department at the University of Cape Town, is not devoted to remedial language communication drills, I am not claiming that it focuses exclusively on the study of literature. It is formally a department of "English Language and Literature." In common with many departments in South Africa and the United Kingdom as well as in most countries where English is taught as a foreign language, UCT's English department houses a linguistics faculty, which offers a set of basic introductory courses (Introduction to Language Studies and Introduction to Applied Language Studies) as well as its own separate concentrations and programs both within the undergraduate major and at the level of higher degrees. At UCT, the major in linguistics, though offered through the English department, is quite distinct from the major in English, with no overlapping requirements. In fact, since students in the humanities at UCT must choose two majors, each involving 6 of the minimum 20 semester-long classes required for the 3-year bachelor of arts degree, only students who choose to combine their English major with linguistics (rather than with, say, art history, drama, or film studies) would be likely to take any linguistics classes at all. In relative terms, the BA program in English is much larger; only two of the department's 20 permanent faculty are specialists in linguistics, and literature courses dominate the elective offerings. It is thus far more common for linguistics majors to choose some of their electives from the literature offerings than for the English majors to choose electives in linguistics. An English major would more likely choose from the wider array of electives in film, media, or creative writing.

115

There is nothing anomalous about the relationship between literature and language study at UCT, and yet one hesitates to say it is typical, even of comprehensive research universities in South Africa. In the RSA as in many countries, the organization of tracks, concentrations, majors, departments, faculties, and schools is surprisingly variable, and the literary and linguistic approaches to English are parceled out in many different ways across these institutional divisions. At the University of KwaZulu-Natal, for example, the BA in English studies is offered by the School of Literary Studies, Media, and Creative Arts, while the first degree in linguistics is a BS, offered by the School of Language, Literature, and Linguistics. Though still much smaller than the literature section, linguistics at KwaZulu-Natal boasts a larger faculty and significantly more course offerings than at UCT, and its degree programs are set up differently. It is still possible for students to do a joint major in the two fields, but they must indicate a subject and a school of primary emphasis so as to receive either a BA (in recognition of their attainments in the liberal arts of literary and cultural study) or a BS (based on their more specialized work in linguistics and language development).

The different departmental configurations in these two South African universities point to a first major zone of variability among the world's English departments: the extent to which they incorporate English linguistics and language study. There are universities, even entire national systems, where courses in English language study and/or linguistic theory constitute half or more of the required credits for an English baccalaureate degree. And there are other universities in other countries where the English BA curriculum is entirely free of all such requirements and where even electives in these fields are scarce or non-existent. I will briefly survey here some of the prevalent curricular models with respect to the "language studies" component of English studies – touching only on a few of the more illuminating or statistically significant locations around the world, but with particular emphasis on the case of China. I will then proceed with similarly rapid and partial surveys of the two other key areas of variability in the discipline's undergraduate curricula, namely "culture studies" (with emphasis on Europe and Australia) and "creative writing" (with emphasis on the United States and the United Kingdom). Along the way I will be sketching the contours of the curriculum in English literature itself. The literary component of the discipline is by no means identical in every location, and even where there is a text in common there may be wide variation in the way that text is approached at different universities and in different countries. In general, the more culturally and linguistically foreign the material, the more formalist and structuralist the approach; new historicism at Berkeley, narratology in Beijing. But at the undergraduate level, a kind of ad hoc thematic criticism, involving close attention to particular passages of text, seems to have installed itself as a global pedagogical orthodoxy. And as regards the curriculum itself, there is less divergence than we might imagine from the canon of classic British and American works. Moreover, as I will stress in what follows, the place of this canonical literary study within the baccalaureate degree program as a whole – the total number of classroom hours spent studying distinguished works of fiction, drama, and poetry – is surprisingly uniform throughout the world.

My four divisions – literary studies, language studies, culture studies, and creative writing – are deliberately broad. What I am calling language studies could readily be divided in two; there are institutions where language learning is a big part of the English degree program but linguistics is not, and vice versa. Indeed, as we will see, the language piece of the English curriculum could be broken down into still finer subcategories: rhetoric and composition, communications, English teaching methods, translation studies, and more. "Culture studies" might be subdivided into cultural history, area studies, (British) cultural studies, film and media studies, and more. Creative writing might be divided between traditional workshops in fiction, nonfiction, drama, or poetry and more strictly vocational training in "writing for the media." Literary studies itself might be divided into British, American, and Anglophone literature; literary theory and critical methods; and any number of specific approaches and thematic

117

emphases (e.g., literature and gender, literature and Marxism, or literature and the material text). But the point of this part of the book is to provide a quick, wide-angle picture of English studies around the world, and in particular to gauge the size and complexion of the literary piece of the curriculum. To capture fine points of difference between, say, the position of the subfield of "law and literature" in Western European English departments versus American ones – even if one could overcome the difficulties of varying nomenclature and the near total lack of relevant datasets – would muddy that picture rather than enhancing it.[13]

To begin, then, with the study of language. The discipline's involvement in this area, particularly in English linguistics, is greatest in the traditional European departments, where the old philological model of the national language and national literature still to a great extent obtains, such that linguistics faculty and literary faculty remain bound together institutionally within departments that are devoted to teaching verbal and written proficiency in a foreign language as well as its history, linguistic structure, and literature. Linguists and literary scholars in these departments of "modern language and literature" share students, and both offer introductory courses required of all undergraduate majors.[14]

The involvement of English departments in language and linguistics curricula is probably least in the United States, where although the traditional rubric "language and literature" remains the departmental designation at many institutions, most departments are very little engaged in teaching such areas as language structure, morphology and phonology, or even history of the English language. As the ADE Ad Hoc Committee on the English Major observed in a 2003 report, while these were once standard areas of coverage in American English departments, "the formal study of the language itself (grammar, philology-linguistics) has [now generally] been abandoned or ceded to another unit."[15] At most US universities today, students interested in linguistics fulfill their core requirements entirely outside the English department, and are as likely to seek their electives in such disciplines as psychology, mathematics, or information sciences as in literature.

With respect to this first axis of differentiation, then, the world's English departments can be roughly mapped between two paradigms: the European "language and literature" model, in which training in language and linguistics is a normal part of the English degree program, and the American "English literature" model, in which language and linguistics are taught outside the discipline and form no significant part of the requirements for an English BA. Before attempting to sketch such a map, however, we need to acknowledge three complications in this simple schematic.

First, as I have indicated, the language component in the English curriculum is much broader than a single term like "linguistics" can suggest, encompassing various vocationally oriented classes as well as the kinds of remedial communication-skills classes that are satirized by Coetzee. Depending on what kind of university houses it, and in which country or region, an English department may be expected to offer courses not only in the history and structure of English and in the theory of language, but also in such areas as speech, communications, rhetoric and composition, professional English (e.g., English for Specific Purposes, English for the Law, and English for Technical Careers), English translation, English education, and Teaching English as a Foreign Language (TEFL). These last two point toward a major driver of the whole language side of the discipline, from the courses in descriptive grammar and rhetorical analysis to those in written communication. The substantial curricular acreage occupied by these kinds of classes in many of the world's English departments is owing less to any residual fascination with philological scholarship or to rising student demand for the excitements of applied linguistics than to the fact that the most common professional destination for English majors nearly everywhere is primary and secondary school teaching, that is, teaching not exclusively of literature but of "language arts." In China, the number of majors heading to teaching careers has been estimated at more than a third; in some European countries, it is more than 50%.[16] The role of English studies as a global base for teacher training, coupled with the rise of English as a required foreign language in many of the world's primary and secondary school systems (systems that are themselves collectively expanding toward the goal of universal education),[17] has partly determined the discipline's curricular accommodation of applied linguistics, TEFL, English grammar, and so forth, just as it has partly determined the gender tilt of its student population, which is two thirds or more female practically everywhere.[18] And the American model, in which English departments are relatively – though of course far from entirely – sequestered from the units that handle communication, education, EFL, and even writing (composition being among the areas that have been widely "abandoned or ceded" to units outside the discipline) is partly a function of the relatively low percentage of US English majors who become teachers: only 15%, according to the most recent MLA study.[19]

A second complication: even in the United States and in Europe, there is very imperfect conformity with either of our two models. As noted in the case of South Africa, divisional and curricular arrangements tend to vary from one university to another within the same country. Though the general rule in the United States is that colleges and universities have located courses in communication, education, English language training, TESL/TEFL, and so on, outside of their English departments, there are many exceptions. With respect to education, for example, there may be wide variance even within a single state university system, with the qualifications for teaching English at the secondary level earned in accordance with what I am calling the "American" model at one institution and the "European" model at another. Consider Iowa's university system. At the flagship University of Iowa, students seeking licensure in English education must enroll in both the College of Liberal Arts and Sciences, which houses the English department, and the College of Education, eventually earning a combined degree. They fulfill all their vocational requirements in the Education school, covering such areas as linguistics, rhetoric, English teaching, and TEFL. Meanwhile, under the umbrella of Liberal Arts and Sciences, they fulfill the normal requirements for an English major in an English department that teaches no classes at all in those vocational areas. At Iowa State University, on the other hand, the English department offers its own courses toward fulfillment of the BA in English Education, as well as offering other degree tracks that require some of the same courses in English language and communication. Students may, for example, choose English with emphasis in rhetorical studies, which features a balanced curriculum of literature and language study, or they may enroll, still under the English department's administrative auspices, in a BA program in speech communication or a BS program in rhetoric and professional communication, programs that have practically no requirements involving literary studies.

The variability of programs increases further as we look beyond bachelor's degree programs at the wider "service" curriculum provided by English instructional staff. My emphasis in this study is on English studies at the baccalaureate level: the curriculum of a typical bachelor's degree-seeking English major in today's higher educational system. But that curriculum represents a smaller or larger portion of a department's instructional load depending on the nature of the institution. And this brings us to the third complication involved in the global mapping of language versus literature. The institutional distance between an English department and the curricula of language, linguistics, rhetoric, education, and communication tends to correlate with institutional status, with the more privileged universities (University of Iowa) housing English departments devoted more exclusively to literary studies and producing graduates more likely to pursue careers in law or business than in teaching. At somewhat lower-status institutions (Iowa State), English departments tend to assume more of the burden of teaching language and communications classes, and to feature BA programs in which a modest language component is included among the core requirements. Another example of this latter sort would be CUNY's Staten Island campus, where the English Department staffs a cluster of remedial (zero-level) classes in reading and writing as well as two general education (100-level) classes in college writing, these being classes primarily for students outside the English major. Within the major, there is an Introduction to Language as well as an Introduction to Literature, and there is even an optional linguistics track leading to the English BA. But all majors are expected to take at least half their credits in literature classes, which in any case dominate the course offerings at the 200- and 300-level. If we drill down further through the tertiary system to the institutions that cannot even offer a bachelor's degree (and so do not contribute at all to our enrollment figures in Part I), we find English departments, or sometimes programs, whose curriculum consists almost entirely of language-focused courses in remedial reading, composition, and professional communication, and in which English *majors* are scarce or non-existent.

The correlation between the language component and institutional status holds true, after a fashion, even in countries where English is not the medium of instruction, general or liberal arts requirements are not a normal part of the baccalaureate curriculum, and cohabitation of literary studies with language studies is not the exception but the rule. At the leading, world-ranked universities in such countries, though English departments continue to teach an array of classes in the history and theory of language and to offer prominent degree tracks in linguistics, it is becoming common to establish a separate center or program to handle the less academically legitimate, more strictly vocational forms of English language study. An example is the highly regarded National University of Singapore, where a Centre for English Language Communication has been set up to teach courses like Business and Technical Communication or Law Intensive English, leaving the linguists in the English Department to teach such areas as Discourse Analysis, Semantics and Pragmatics, and Bilingualism. For reasons I will discuss further below, I believe this tendency to remove basic or vocational language instruction from the English curriculum as such will spread, or indeed is already spreading, beyond the elite universities. But the point here – the third complication in our mapping of the language-literature relationship – is that one could just as well compose the map vertically, through the economic and status hierarchies of the global university system, as horizontally, across its national and geographic locations. As we know, the world's higher educational apparatus is becoming more integrated, easing the movement of students, faculty, credits, and credentials across national and regional borders. But the form this integration is taking is such that the top- and bottom-tier universities within a country are gradually coming to resemble similarly situated institutions abroad more closely than they do each other.

I will focus for the moment, however, on the geographical aspect, which has not yet lost its relevance for English degree programs. Some countries do conform pretty closely and predictably to one or the other of the two basic paradigms. China, for example, follows the European pattern, with English departments typically housed in schools or divisions devoted to foreign languages and literatures (or modern languages and literatures), requiring all students to take introductory courses in linguistics as well as in literature, and even in rare cases offering the option to choose a concentration or track through the more advanced semesters of the program that emphasizes language over literature. This would typically be a track in English linguistics, English translation, or some version of what is known in this context as "English Plus" (English in support of another discipline).

This is as we would expect in a country with an enormous student population and almost no native speakers of English. We find similar conformity with the original Western European pattern in Brazil and other countries of Latin America, as well as in Scandinavia and most countries of post-Soviet Europe. But English is now an "official language" in more than 50 countries, what Braj Kachru calls the "outer circle" of global English, between the "inner circle" of Anglophone nations and the "expanding circle" where English is an unofficial lingua franca.[20] In many of these outer-circle countries – particularly the ones whose education systems were developed under the auspices of British imperial policy – the status of English as a "foreign language" is not so clear. As we've seen, the place of language studies in the English program is highly variable in South Africa, where only 8% of the population speaks English at home yet the higher educational apparatus is firmly Anglophone. In India, where English has been the main medium of instruction at research universities and many of their affiliated colleges since the nineteenth century, there are relatively few English departments housing linguists or offering tracks in language and linguistics. In Hong Kong and Taiwan, on the other hand, despite comparably long histories of Anglophone instruction, English departments tend to be configured much like those in Mainland China, offering a bachelor's program with dual core requirements (Introduction to Linguistics and Introduction to Literary Studies) followed by a choice of literary or linguistic emphases at the elective level. In Singapore, both models are evident, though even the departments that encompass linguistics as well as literature (e.g., National University of Singapore, but not Nanyang Technical University) keep the two degree programs entirely separate, with no courses in the one area required of students pursuing degrees in the other.

In Canada, with its dual linguistic heritages, the situation is less predictable still. Outside of Quebec, English and linguistics are almost always separated as in the United States.[21] The universities of la francophonie are more likely to conform to the European pattern, as for example is the case at the Université de Sherbrooke. But even among the Francophone universities there are a number, such as Université Laval and the Université de Montréal, that feature free-standing English literature departments and separate departments of language, linguistics, and translation. This lack of uniformity is in fact typical of many countries, including the United Kingdom itself, where we find departments defined in accord with both of the dominant templates as well as along various compromise lines.[22] At Oxford, the English Department has nothing to do with linguistics, which is housed in the Faculty of Linguistics, Philology, and Phonetics. Similar separation of the two faculties is found at the nearby former polytechnic, Oxford Brookes University, and at many others such as the universities of Manchester and Essex. Some of these universities offer a dual degree in English literature and linguistics, with students taking half their courses in one school and half in the other (the same arrangement as at KwaZulu-Natal in South Africa). The joint-degree option is also available at Cambridge, but with no bridging required between schools, as Applied Linguistics is set up (rather ambiguously) as a "freestanding but subsidiary departmental unit" within the Faculty of English. Further along in the direction of the European foreign language model are the schools of "English literature, language, and linguistics" at such universities as Sheffield and Newcastle, where students choose between a bachelor's degree track in English literature, an integrated track in language and literature, or a distinct track in language and linguistics (with little or no required coursework in literature).

If we confine our view to the Anglophone sphere, these varied curricular options in language studies affect only a small fraction of the enrollment figures in English degree programs. Linguistics faculty tend to be greatly outnumbered by literary faculty, and courses in language studies are scarce in comparison with courses in literature. A 2003 survey found that less than half of UK English departments offer the option of a mixed language-literature emphasis.[23] As those departments are also offering four or five other possible tracks through the English BA program (all of them centered on literature), we can estimate that the language-literature option involves less than 10% of the country's English majors. And even the students doing these integrated programs would generally have more literature than language courses among their electives, on top of the introductory literature courses required of all majors. As for students concentrating wholly in English language studies, with few or no courses in literature, these represent a negligible fraction of total English BA enrollments. According to the same UK survey, only 15% of the departments even offer a distinct track in language and linguistics, and anecdotal evidence suggests it is a very narrow track, running along the far fringes of the major. (At Sheffield, for example, it is the least popular of the five undergraduate course options.)

The situation is similar in the United States, where although linguistics as such is not an option for English BA students, about 15% of them concentrate in the area classified by the NCES as "Speech and Rhetorical Studies."[24] An example of the kind of program included in this category is the English BA with concentration in rhetoric and composition at the University of Georgia. According to the university's catalog, the program "emphasizes critical thinking, articulate self-expression, and a broad knowledge of English and American Literature, language history and usage, and the critical contexts that help us to interpret our own age as well as others." Nearly all such programs involve both core requirements and electives in literary studies, and there are practically none that allow students to focus exclusively on language studies.

Overall, we might estimate that some 10% of officially reported English BA recipients in the United Kingdom, Canada, Australia, and the United States are students whose primary curricular emphasis is on language study rather than literature. And this number would be at least partially offset by students receiving bachelor's degrees in linguistics, comparative literature, communication studies, and so on who in fact earned most of their credits in English literature classes.

Things are different outside the Anglophone core, where the various requirements and curricular options focused on language and linguistics – including classes in English listening and speaking, English translation, and teaching English as a foreign language – naturally represent a much larger share of the reported bachelor's degrees in English. Nevertheless, it is a mistake to assume that, outside of the United States, the United Kingdom, and other English-language countries, the curriculum of the English major consists primarily of courses in the history, structure, practical use, and teaching of the English language – that majoring in English essentially means learning the language rather than the literature.

China: English Plus, Literature Minus?

As the largest producer of English BAs outside the Anglophone sphere, China warrants our particular attention here. When people hear that China now has more English majors than the United States, their immediate response is that those cannot be "real"

English majors: they must be students doing basic English language studies – the Chinese version of David Lurie's students in Communications 101. And, to be sure, classes in English language training (ELT) are abundant and exceedingly heavily enrolled throughout the Chinese system. Basic proficiency in English is required for admission to college, and proficiency at a higher level or "band" of examinations is required for graduation. ELT is thus a required, practical, and vocational component of all majors, dumping vast student populations into basic service courses which, unless a separate center has been established for the purpose, can all but overwhelm an English department and overshadow its more specialized teaching in the academic subject of English literature. At the prestigious Tsinghua University in Beijing, for example, the English faculty within the Foreign Language Department face enrollments of nearly 4000 students a year in a service class called English Speaking, Listening, and Writing, with several thousand more taking either English for Academic Purposes or English for Specific Purposes.[25] Such courses constitute a complex burden for the department – roughly analogous to the required freshman composition and "developmental" (remedial) writing classes at many US universities – and they are similarly handled by a large instructional staff (the English Learning Environment Group) that toils at the very bottom of the faculty employment ladder, below the main rungs of lecturer, associate professor and professor. But these kinds of courses should not be conflated with the curriculum of the English major itself.[26] Though dwarfed in scale by the ELT enrollments, the English BA program at Tsinghua is a substantial enterprise, admitting 80 students a year (about 2.5 percent of the university's entering class) for 4 years of study in linguistics and professional communication, British and American literature, and electives in related fields of the liberal arts.[27] The English faculty within the Department of Foreign Languages consists of 15 full professors, 9 associate professors, and a number of lecturers, whose teaching time is divided between the roughly 300 BA students and about 120 graduate students (mostly 3-year MA candidates). And while the curriculum for the undergraduates is rudimentary by Anglophone standards, it is undeniably — and, it appears, increasingly — literary in orientation.

The core requirements for a BA in English studies in China are guided by a National Curriculum set down by the Ministry of Education, and are roughly balanced between classroom hours devoted to language learning, linguistics and translation, and literature. The standard 4-year degree program begins with two "skills" years consisting mostly of required courses in English language study (e.g., comprehension, listening, speaking, reading, and writing) and usually including an Introduction to Linguistics and an Introduction to Translation. Typically the only required literature class in the freshman or sophomore year would be a general introduction to literary studies or to world literature, which might be taught in Chinese rather than English. But after this initial period of language training, many of the core requirements are in literary studies, generally including a yearlong survey in British literature for juniors and a yearlong survey in American literature for seniors. Electives vary from one university to another, with the most distinguished departments featuring the widest range of elective offerings. But all departments offer electives in the area of language and linguistics as well as in literature; many also offer courses in translation and in something like "General English" or "College English" — a flexible mixed curriculum for students taking courses also in a second discipline, pursuing the equivalent of a US double major or a UK joint honours degree. These different subfields of English studies are rarely presented as distinct tracks or formal "concentrations" at the undergraduate level; only MA and doctoral students must choose a specific track. BA students tend to mix electives from all areas so that even those most strongly oriented toward translation studies or linguistics will end up with perhaps a quarter to a third of their overall curriculum in English being classes in literary study, while for students more oriented toward literature the credits in literary studies would approach half the classes in the major.

What does this amount to in terms of the actual number of courses and credits in English literature? It depends on a number of factors, including how closely the university has fashioned itself on the American liberal arts model (in which English majors face broad distribution requirements in the social and natural sciences) versus the European model (in which English majors concentrate narrowly on the major subject or subjects). It is possible, however, to indicate a roughly average load. Like most universities outside the United Kingdom and Europe, Chinese universities quantify course credits according to classroom hours, with a typical class meeting 2 to 4 hours a week and counting for 2 to 4 credits. But many universities in China treat different components of a class (e.g. the speaking, writing, and listening portions of a foreign language class) as separate courses, resulting in classes that count for just a single credit or even half a credit. And at the other end of the spectrum there are specially demanding classes counting 5 or even 6 credits. Whether 1 credit or 6, students have told me that the credits do not perfectly correlate with the actual number of classroom hours. But there's no doubt that college students in China take more classes than elsewhere: as many as 10 or 12 per semester. National guidelines require a minimum of 2000 hours for a BA, which translates to 125 credits (assuming 16-week semesters), but many universities require more. At Tsinghua, for example, the minimum is 140; at Huazhong Normal it is 150, and this is by no means the top of the range. Total classroom hours may thus be as high as 2500, of which about half, on average, would be in the major subject or related subjects required for the major. The remaining classes would include about 25 credits' worth of compulsory "public courses" in such subjects as Marxism, Maoism, and PE, as well as a variable number of general-knowledge credits that must be earned outside of the major.

The upshot is that an English major at a Chinese university might complete anywhere between 20 and 45 credits in literary studies, out of about 50 to 100 in the major. This is equivalent to about 300 to 600 classroom hours of literary study. By way of illustration, Figure 3.1 reproduces the transcript of an English major who graduated in 2004 from Huazhong Normal University – a respectable but not an elite or especially internationalized or

ACADEMIC RECORD OF GRADUATE AT

HUAZHONG NORMAL UNIVERSITY

Name:
Number:

Dept.: Foreign Languages
Specialty: English

Length of Schooling: Four Years
Date of Enrollment: Sep. 2000

Courses	Record/Credit	Term	Courses	Record/Credit	Term
College Physical Education (1)	78/1	1	Anthropology	75/2	5
Mind and Moral Cultivation	73/3	1	Keeping Fresh of Fruits, Vegetables and Flowers	73/2	5
Introduction to Maoist Thought	82/3	1	Introduction to Sexology	77/2	5
Comprehensive English 1A	86/3	1	Introduction to Deng Xiaoping Theory	75/4	5
Listing 1A	76/1	1	Comprehensive English 3A	82/3	5
Grammar A	86/2	1	Audio-Visual Course A	80/2	5
Intonation A	79/1	1	Translation Theory and Technique A	86/2	5
Language Practice 1A	93/1	1	Introduction to English Linguistics	91/2	5
Elementary Course of Computer	86/4	1	The Second Foreign Language 1 (French)	90/4	5
College Chinese	80/2	2	English Literature Appreciation	88/2	5
College Physical Education (2)	80/1	2	History of British Literature	86/2	5
Elementary Course of Law	74/2	2	Educational Technology	81/3	6
Comprehensive English 1B	81/3	2	Go	70/2	6
Listing 1B	88/1	2	Contemporary World Economics and Politics	84/2	6
Grammar B	79/2	2	Literary Theory and Criticism	82/2	6
Intonation B	77/1	2	Comparative Literature	82/2	6
Language Practice 1B	90/1	2	English Teaching Methodology	82/3	6
Courseware Design	85/2	2	Comprehensive English 3B	88/3	6

Course	Credits	Grade	Course	Grade	Credits
College Physical Education (3)	3	78/1	Audio-Visual Course B	74/2	6
Principles of Marxist Philosophy	3	84/3	Translation Theory and Technique B	87/2	6
Psychology	3	82/3	The Second Foreign Language 2 (French)	86/4	6
Comprehensive English 2A	3	87/3	Appreciation of Classical English Movies	88/2	6
Listing 2A	3	84/2	History of American Literature	83/2	6
Language Practice 2A	3	88/1	Interpretation	78/2	6
Reading 2A	3	82/2	Comprehensive English 4A	78/3	7
Writing A	3	87/2	British Literature	96/2	7
College Physical Education (4)	4	77/1	American Literature	85/2	7
Marxist Political Economy	4	78/2	The Second Foreign Language 3 (French)	87/3	7
Pedagogy	4	80/3	Introduction to English Literature	84/2	7
Comprehensive English 2B	4	85/3	Modern English Drama	87/2	7
Listing 2B	4	83/2	Comprehensive English 4B	80/3	8
Language Practice 2B	4	92/1	The Second Foreign Language 4 (French)	85/3	8
Reading 2B	4	76/2	Modern American Novel	89/2	8
Writing B	4	87/2	Selected Plays of Shakespeare	87/2	8
Introductory Course to the Great Britain and America	4	72/2	Education Practice	Good/6	
History of Western Thought and Culture	4	89/2	Graduation Thesis	Good/6	
			GPA of Total Courses	82.75	

Figure 3.1 **Transcript for 2004 English BA recipient in China.**

Source: Huazhong Normal University.

Americanized institution.[28] Of 94 credits the student took within the major (somewhat more than half of the total credits toward the BA), 30 were in literary studies, 2 in British and American culture, 2 in classic American film, and the rest in language learning, linguistics, translation, and pedagogy. Even if we omit the 6 credits earned for the undergraduate thesis in literature (since this work did not involve actual class time), this is still about 380 classroom hours of literary study. With the thesis work included, the figure would be 480 hours.

As I will be detailing in what follows, this is not so far as we might think from the international norm. In terms of total classroom hours, the literary component of the English major in China is comparable to that in most European systems, where students in a 3-year English BA program might be expected to take about a quarter of their 1400 hours in English literature courses, most of the rest being in language and linguistics and in a second major subject. Nor is it much different in the United States, where the core literary requirements plus electives taken in literary studies (rather than cultural or media studies or creative writing) would, at a conservative estimate, average out to eight courses or 400 hours per student, about 20% of the class time typically required for a baccalaureate degree.[29] Even in the United Kingdom, where the language and linguistics component of English is much smaller than in China or Europe, and where the curriculum is much less spread out into general requirements and nonmajor electives than in the United States, the gap is not as wide as we might imagine. A UK English major would typically take a higher proportion of classes in literary studies than students elsewhere, but as the standard BA program is only 3 years and total contact hours generally around 1000, the literary component would still be less than 500 classroom hours.[30] The figure would be higher for students doing a four-year BA but lower for students doing joint-honours degrees.

The reasons for this somewhat surprising equivalency of the course load in literature are not hard to discern. Chinese students take more classes per term than students in most other countries

(10 vs. an average of 4 or 5), they complete 8 terms of coursework rather than the 6 that are standard in many countries, and they consequently spend more time in the classroom than baccalaureate students elsewhere. The transcript in Figure 3.1 represents 2400 hours of class time; nearly all Chinese students complete 2000 hours or more, versus a global average of 1200–1500. Just as important, apart from language training (generally at least 150 hours a year) and linguistics, translation, and pedagogy courses (another 100 hours a year), English departments in China tend not to offer many courses in the discipline's main subfields. In some of the European programs, as I will discuss in a moment, "language" and "literature" are triangulated with "civilization" via required courses in American and/or British cultural and political history. Such courses are generally a very minor presence in China's English departments. The basic skills classes do sometimes rely on textbooks that present social and political issues (racism, unequal education, gun ownership, globalization, climate change) through brief readings in classic or contemporary British and American journalism.[31] And there might be a general introduction to Britain and America, in addition to a college-wide elective introduction to Western culture. But only at a few very prestigious universities, where the English BA program has been consciously configured along international lines, do we find such classes beyond the introductory level, and even these universities would not have systematic modules in history and civilization or any interdisciplinary form of area studies integrated into the English major.[32]

Also comparatively rare in China are courses in TV and media studies, digital entertainment studies, or the other fields of broadly "cultural" study that have become part of the English curriculum of many departments in Australia, the United States, and elsewhere. Movies are frequently used in classes on speaking and listening, and there might in some departments be an elective course on Hollywood films, but film studies as a developed branch or mode of English studies has barely a toehold in China. And the other most prominent broad track or option within English studies worldwide, creative writing, is likewise almost unheard of in China, appearing only in the form of an occasional pedagogical experiment in language training.[33]

The relative absence of these other options and alternatives means that, apart from classes in language studies (including linguistics and pedagogy), classes in literature fill out the major. The literature classes, moreover, are quite traditional, rather more so than in the United States – reflecting, like other sites of English studies remote from the major hubs, a time lag with respect to the process of canon revision. The time lag is perhaps widened in China's case by the role of the Ministry of Education, whose national curriculum for College English leaves room for variability among the different kinds of institution and the different strengths of particular faculties but tends to be infrequently revised and so to impose rather static guidelines. There is for example a list of about a hundred British and American novels, which provides the basis for syllabi in most advanced fiction classes in China. Looking at the British portion of the list (Figure 3.2), one notes in the later twentieth century some authors who were more studied a few decades ago than they are now in the United States and the United Kingdom (e.g., Ivy Compton-Burnett, Somerset Maugham, and John Fowles) while authors who have been widely taught and discussed in recent years (Jean Rhys, George Lamming, Kazuo Ishiguro, and Zadie Smith) are absent. But if the lineup might strike an English major in London – or even, for that matter, in Shanghai – as slightly out of date, it is otherwise a perfectly standard list of classics in English fiction, reflecting no imposition of an unfamiliar, foreign scale of value. Defoe and Austen, Dickens and Eliot, Woolf and Joyce, Rushdie and Carter: this would be the foundation of a sound training in the English novel practically anywhere.

Not that undergraduates at Peking University, much less at Xihua or Sechuan Normal or other provincial universities, are actually reading their way through *Middlemarch*. The national list is more or less aspirational, pointing toward a canon with which most English BA students will only just begin to familiarize themselves, learning authors' names and titles, historical periods and

134

Author	Work(s)
Kingsley Amis	Lucky Jim
Jane Austen	Pride and Prejudice
Arnold Bennett	The Old Wives' Tale
Elizabeth Bowen	The Death of the Heart
Charlotte Brontë	Jane Eyre
Emily Brontë	Wuthering Heights
Anthony Burgess	A Clockwork Orange
Samuel Butler	The Way of All Flesh
A. S. Byatt	Possession
Lewis Carroll	Alice's Adventures in Wonderland
Angela Carter	The Company of Wolves
Agatha Christie	Murder on the Orient Express
Ivy Compton-Burnett	A Family and a Fortune
Joseph Conrad	Heart of Darkness / Lord Jim
Daniel Dafoe	Robinson Crusoe
Charles Dickens	David Copperfield
Sir Arthur C. Doyle	The Adventures of Sherlock Holmes
Margaret Drabble	The Waterfall
Daphne Du Maurier	Rebecca
George Eliot	Middlemarch
E. M. Forster	Howards End / A Passage to India
John Fowles	The French Lieutenant's Woman
John Galsworthy	The Man of Property
William Golding	Lord of the Flies
Graham Greene	The Human Factor
Thomas Hardy	Tess of the D'Urbervilles / Jude the Obscure
Aldous Huxley	After Many a Summer
Henry James	Daisy Miller
James Joyce	A Portrait of the Artist as a Young Man
Rudyard Kipling	Kim
Charles Lamb	Tales from Shakespeare
D. H. Lawrence	Sons and Lovers
John Le Carre	The Spy Who Came in from the Cold
Doris Lessing	The Grass is Singing
David Lodge	Nice Work
W. Somerset Maugham	The Moon and Sixpence / Of Human Bondage
Iris Murdoch	The Black Prince
George Orwell	Nineteen Eighty-four
Salman Rushdie	Midnight's Children
Sir Walter Scott	Ivanhoe
C. P. Snow	The Affair
Muriel Spark	The Prime of Miss Jean Brodie
Robert Louis Stevenson	Treasure Island
Jonathan Swift	Gulliver's Travels
William M. Thackeray	Vanity Fair
Evelyn Waugh	A Handful of Dust
H. G. Wells	The Invisible Man
Oscar Wilde	The Picture of Dorian Gray
Virginia Woolf	Mrs Dalloway / To the Lighthouse

Figure 3.2 Reading list in the British novel, from the Chinese national curriculum.

Source: Ministry of Education of the People's Republic of China, *College English* (Shanghai: Shanghai Foreign Language Education Press, 2000, 2009).

genres, and basic formal and narrative features of particular works. Actual reading assignments consist mostly of excerpts, presented along with historical and biographical headnotes, vocabulary lists, and study questions, in readers or textbooks, which form the backbone of the English curriculum in China. Typical of such books is *Selected Readings in English Literature*, published by Shanghai Jiao Tong University Press and used in some third-year British lit surveys. (See Figure 3.3.) Aside from lyric poems, the selections in this volume consist of very brief snippets: just 200 lines from Act IV of *The Merchant of Venice* and fewer than 10 pages from *Oliver Twist, Vanity Fair, Mrs Dalloway, Portrait of the Artist,* and other novels drawn from the national curriculum.

Only students who continue on to the 2- and 3-year English MA programs are likely to graduate from these kinds of textbooks and begin reading major literary works in their entirety. This is not a negligible cohort; the MA in English is a more respected and more heavily enrolled degree program in China than in any Anglophone country. But even the bachelor's curriculum aims at more than simply developing proficiency in the English language; it is designed to teach students about the literary traditions of Britain, United States, and (to a lesser extent) the postcolonial sphere, and to develop their facility in working with literary language and the tools of literary criticism. Training in English literature is a strong emphasis in the curriculum even for students whose interests and career goals tend more in the direction of language arts or translation.

There are also indications that the literary component of the BA may be expanding as a result of the country's ongoing and dramatic linguistic transformation. English has been a compulsory subject at the secondary level in China since the mid-1990s, and at the primary level since 2001, with primary schools required to introduce the language no later than the third grade, and many starting in year 1.[34] Since the early 2000s, middle-class families in the major cities have even begun sending their toddlers to English-language preschools and kindergartens, where the teachers are typically native speakers, often Australian or Canadian ex-pats. At the same

136

Chapter One: The English Renaissance (1500–1625)	
Introduction to the Background	1
William Shakespeare	4
Sonnet 18	5
The Merchant of Venice	6
Chapter Two: The Seventeenth Century (1625–1700)	
Introduction the Background	15
John Donne	17
A Valediction: Forbidding Mourning	18
Sonnet 10	20
John Milton	21
Paradise Lost	23
Chapter Three: The Eighteenth Century (1700–1798)	
Introduction to the Background	27
Daniel Defoe	30
The Life and strange Surprising Adventures of Robinson Cr	31
Robert Burns	40
Selected Poems	42
William Blake	46
Selected Poems	47
Chapter Four: The Romantic Period (1798–1832)	
Introduction to the Background	50
William Wordsworth	54
Selected Poems	55
Percy Bysshe Shelley	58
Ode to the West Wind	59
John Keats	63
Ode to a Nightingale	64
Jave Austen	68
Emma	69
Chapter Five: The Victorian Age (1832–1901)	
Introduction to the Background	81
Charles Dickens	85
Oliver Twist	87
William Makepeace Thackeray	100
Vanity Fair	101
Emily Brontë	110
Wuthering Heights	111
Thomas Hardy	125
Tess of the D'Urbervilles	126
The Darkling Thrush	135
Chapter Six: The Twentieth Century (1900–)	
Introduction to the Background	138
Joseph Conrad	141
Heart of Darkness	143
William Butler Yeats	156
The Second Coming	157
Thomas stearns Eliot	159
The Love song of J. Alfred Prufrock	160
James Joyce	167
A Portrait of the Artist as a Young Man	168
D. H. Lawrence	179
Women in Love	180
Katherine Mansfield	192
The Garden Party	193
Virginia Woolf	206
Mrs Dalloway	207
Edward Morgan Forster	216
A Passage to India	217
Samuel Beckett	230
Waiting for Godot	231
William Golding	243
Lord of the flies	245
John Fowles	253
The French Lieutenant's Woman	255
Doris Lessing	269
A Road to the Big City	270

Figure 3.3 Table of contents from a Chinese anthology of British literature.

Source: Wang Song Nian, ed., *Selected Readings in English Literature* (Shanghai: Shanghai Jiao Tong University Press, 2003).

time, the proliferation of personal computers and the rise of digital media have made British and American films, TV programs, websites, and other Anglophone media products a part of mainstream youth culture in China as throughout the world, extending opportunities to acquire English fluency well beyond the moneyed classes. The upshot is that more and more students are arriving at Chinese universities with better English proficiency than the graduates of just a few years ago, better indeed than many faculty, who in a system that has grown as rapidly as China's are often seriously under-qualified and whose own educations in English a decade or two ago were comparatively primitive. This is creating a curious inversion of skill levels in many English departments, where the very best English speakers are likely to be undergraduates or younger MA students, followed by the doctoral students, who are in turn more fluent than many of their professors.

Because this generational shift involves the entire college cohort, the rising tide of English fluency has been eroding the linguistic advantage enjoyed by English majors on the job market and softening the once strong employer demand for an English BA credential. A likely consequence will be less interest in the English major not only on the part of students (whose power to choose their field of study in China, though increasing, remains limited) but also on that of the government (which actively manages the size of the various faculties and disciplines). The percentage of Chinese university students pursuing English as their primary field of study will probably decline, even if it continues to rise in absolute terms while the country pushes its gross enrollment ratio up past 30%. But it is also likely that the Anglophone turn across China's whole cultural and educational apparatus will make English studies a livelier and more interesting undergraduate option, attracting more and/or better students into the academic heart of the discipline. Unlike all the other foreign language and literature programs in Chinese universities, which have to bottom-feed from the university application pool, accepting students who have no prior training or background in the language, English enjoys linguistically competent first-year students who are advancing ever more rapidly to serious literary and cultural study. Already observable, at least at the better universities, is a decline of interest in linguistics relative to literature. In some of the departments where students entering the third year choose between two separate tracks, the fraction choosing literature has expanded to two or three times that of linguistics concentrators – bringing China into line with the European English departments.[35] Also evident in China is a kind of creep forward toward the more aspirational end of the national curricular guidelines. The normative 2 years of compulsory coursework in basic language skills is being revised such that literary study may be introduced alongside or as an integral component of the language training.

Thus for example at Nanjing University, students are already reading canonical poetry and fiction in their second-year basic skills course, something that would not have been contemplated a decade ago. The course relies on a new *Introduction to Literature* textbook developed for Shanghai Foreign Language Education Press in 2009 and featuring unabridged short stories by Lawrence, Anderson, Joyce, Hemingway, and Atwood; complete poems by Shakespeare, Browning, Blake, Dickinson, Frost, and Cummings; and readings in literary criticism excerpted from Freud, Williams, Gilbert and Gubar, and Edward Said. The pedagogical apparatus is minimal compared with most first- and second-year readers, consisting mainly of historical and biographical headnotes and sidebar glossaries of difficult words. Peking University is also moving toward a more specifically literary curriculum, using the shorter Norton Anthologies in its survey courses, with for example the survey of American literature, taught by Mao Liang, beginning with the Norton entries for Winthrop, Bradford, Cooper, and Poe. As Professor Mao explained to me, the "old model" for Chinese English departments emphasized general acquaintance with British and American literary culture: the aim was for students to be familiar with important dates, author names, titles, genres, schools, or periods. But the "new model" in place at Peking, Nanjing, and some of the other leading universities "has the goal of close reading the important works."[36] Of course, the departments at

139

these leading universities are not typical. In response to Mao's comments, his colleague Thomas Rendall observed that 90% of China's English departments are still mainly concerned with bringing students' language skills up to standard. But that 90% figure was probably already out of date and is rapidly becoming more so. As regards their accommodation to a more English-proficient student body, departments like those at Nanjing and Peking represent the curricular vanguard. One can expect that the English major in China – already notable for its commitment to the traditional literary canon – will involve significantly more literary study in the future.

Concomitant with this enlargement of the literary component is a trend, already noted in passing, toward the removal of remedial ELT and "English Plus" classes from English departments proper. As English gains status and recognition among the academic disciplines of the humanities in China, there is less call for it to annex itself as a vocational adjunct to more legitimate fields via composite courses like English for law or English for engineers. Already some of the top-ranked departments have withdrawn these kinds of classes from their curricula, offering regular courses in language and literature to students from outside the major, requiring their own majors to take more classes in other disciplines, and widening the institutional aperture for double majors or major-minor combinations – but declining to organize the curriculum in English around perceived verbal deficiencies of students in business, law, or engineering. This is an altogether different model of English Plus, one that involves no "minus," that is, no loss to the integrity of the discipline itself. Not that the other, more pernicious model of English Plus has disappeared from China, any more than it has from other countries. But old-style Plus courses such as Business English are gradually being shifted out of English into the business schools or extra-curricular centers for vocational language training. This is part of a broader shift in the global education system as the world's universities converge around a paradigm that better accommodates student choice, increases curricular breadth and flexibility, and encourages joint-honours, double majors, multiple minors, and individuated degree programs.[37] The new goal is to facilitate the thoughtful selection of courses from different disciplines, rather than to force the aims or interests of one discipline into the curriculum of another.

English Studies and "Culture Studies" in Europe and Australia

This movement toward a common paradigm is nowhere more explicit than in Europe, where the Bologna Process, launched in 1999, has aimed at the convergence of European higher educational institutions upon a single model, with equal requirements for equal degrees and roughly comparable standards of quality across all universities of the "European Higher Education Area." With 47 states now pledging compliance with the Bologna accords, the process has already succeeded in important respects; where a "first degree" once meant quite different things in different countries, the 3- or 4-year bachelor's degree is now effectively universal, making comparison of and mobility between European degree programs much easier. But by unleashing reform in long-static organizational systems, Bologna has fostered all manner of curricular innovations. In the area of literary studies. it has encouraged a range of new interdisciplinary and modular options that are stretching and modifying the traditional "English language and literature" baccalaureate. These developments are welcome on the whole, but they present us with a somewhat dynamic and unstable object of study, with many schools, departments, and faculties of English studies currently in a state of transition.

Nonetheless, certain generalizations may be made. I referred to the curricular arrangements in Chinese English departments as following a European model, and indeed with respect to the language and linguistics component we find a standard set-up in many European universities. Language training is a ubiquitous requirement, averaging about 100 hours per year (3–4 hours per week, or 6–8 "ECTS" credits) for the first 2 years of study, with a minimum of at least 25 hours a year even at the top universities in countries where English skills are generally strong, and ranging upward to about 200 hours a year in the post-Soviet countries, Greece, and some of the other countries where students tend to have less English proficiency at matriculation and where teaching is the expected career path for English BA recipients. The linguistics curriculum is similarly predictable, with both History of the English Language and Phonetics required in nearly every program, and courses in semantics and syntax generally mandatory or strongly encouraged electives. Generative grammar and sociolinguistics are widespread options.[38] Unlike China, where, apart from language learning, most of the first 2 (of 4) years within the major program are devoted to linguistics, in Europe's typical 3-year BA programs, only one of the two introductory years (or half of each year) is devoted to courses in linguistics, the other being reserved for introductions to literary studies and to surveys of British and American literature. The third year typically consists of advanced courses in either or both areas, sometimes arranged into formally separate tracks which majors must choose between. Where such a choice is presented, most students choose literature – at least two thirds in the departments I consulted. As Ina Habermann observed of her experience at various universities in Germany and Switzerland, "linguistics continues to be both an acquired taste and a minority interest."[39]

Another general rule is that in the great majority of European countries, English is routinely combined with a second discipline in some form of double-major or "joint-honours" scheme. In Belgium, Germany, Austria, and at least a dozen more countries, the subject is not even offered as a free-standing degree program; all English students are expected to combine their English studies with parallel study in another discipline, usually in the humanities.[40] The exact configurations of these interdisciplinary programs vary widely and are constantly being adjusted. The general tendency is toward more flexibility, with more subjects being made available for pairing with English, across schools or divisions whose borders were formerly inviolable. Even where options remain limited, they appear to be gradually expanding. In some of the Flemish colleges of Belgium, for example, English language and literature has traditionally been offered as a degree program only in combination with Dutch or German, but lately other modern language and literature programs are being allowed as the second subject, with indications that further options will emerge in due course. At more internationally visible institutions that attract a significant portion of their students from beyond the national borders, English is now offered in combination with dozens of disciplines, including many outside the humanities.

We might very roughly, then, divide the BA curriculum in Europe in half and then in half again, with English studies constituting about half the required degree credits and half of those being composed of linguistics and language studies. Figure 3.4 shows how this breaks down at the University of Basel in Switzerland. Students there take a total of 75 ECTS credits in English out of 180 required, under the terms of the Bologna accords, for a 3-year BA. Another 75–80 credits would be earned in the required second major, and the remaining 30 or so would be either general requirements or free electives (the latter often taken within one or the other major subject). Seventy-five ECTS credits are roughly comparable to 40 semester-hours in the United States, or 13 classes that meet 3 hours a week for a 14-week semester. English majors at Basel who choose the literature track in year three, as more than two thirds of them do, would thus complete, all told, at least 50 hours of language training (more if they lack proficiency), 160 hours of linguistics courses, and 300–400 hours of literature classes, depending on the choice of electives in "related" disciplines within the philosophy, history, and literature division. There would be another 500–600 hours in the second major subject, and 200 more hours to complete the degree (some of which might well be taken within the English literature curriculum). That's around 350 hours of literary studies in a degree program of 1350 classroom hours.

We find ourselves once again hovering around the international average, with about a quarter of the English major's total

Basic Studies			
1st Year			
Course	**Structure**	**ECTS***	**US†**
Learning about Linguistics	2 Lectures with Tutorial (1st yr courses)	8	4
		8	4
Learning about Literature	Proseminar	3	2
	Lecture: "Theories and Methods"	2	1
	Tutorial: "Theories and Methods"	1	1
	Lecture	2	1
		8	5
Practicing English (part 1)	English Language Skills	(3)	(2)
		(3)	(2)
2nd Year			
Course	**Structure**	**ECTS**	**US**
Refining skills in	2 Proseminars (2nd yr courses)	6	3
	Proseminar Work	3	2
	2 Lectures or Tutorials (may include 1 from a related discipline)	4	2
		13	7
Refining Skills in Literature	2 Proseminars (2nd yr courses)	6	3
	Proseminar Work	3	2
	2 Lectures or Tutorials (may include 1 from a related discipline)	4	2
		13	7
Practicing English (part 2)	English Language Skills	(3)	(2)
		(3)	(2)

Studies			
3rd Year: students choose a focus on either literature or linguistics			
Course	**Structure**	**ECTS**	**US**
Focusing on the Discipline	2 seminars	6	3
	Lecture or Tutorial (or guided self-study)	2	1
	Seminar Work	5	3
		13	7
Extending the View	2 Lectures	4	2
	Free choice of courses from English or a related discipline	5	3
		9	5
BA Exam		5	3

* ECTS = European Credit Transfer System units
† US = equiv. US Credits (semester-hours)

Figure 3.4 Curriculum for the BA in English, University of Basel, Switzerland.

Source: "Wegleitung für das Studienfach Englisch im Bachelorstudium," Philosophisch-Historische Fakultät, Universität Basel, May 2008.

undergraduate curriculum devoted to literary studies, just as in the United States, and 300–400 classroom hours, just as in China, the United States, and most other countries. In the less common situation in European universities where English is a stand-alone BA program – for example, in France and the Netherlands – the basic structure of the major is identical, with again equal parts language studies and literary studies in the first 2 years and a choice of emphasis in linguistics or in literature in year three (and most students opting for the latter). The difference is that these single-major programs involve twice as many credits across the board. Figure 3.5 shows the current BA program in English Literature and Culture at the University of Amsterdam. Here, depending on how they use their electives, students who choose the literary emphasis in the third year do approximately 80–100 ECTS credits, or about 600–700 hours.

Both the Basel two-subject degree program and the Amsterdam single-major program include several electives from outside the discipline. These are meant to provide a broader context or framework for literary study, something that Amsterdam also aims to achieve through a required course in *Wetenschapsfilosofie* (appearing in Figure 3.5 as "Foundations of the Humanities"), which covers the basics of literary and cultural theory as they relate to humanistic study in general. More typical is a course or small module of courses in a relevant national "civilization" or "culture": examples culled from catalogs include American Civilization, Introduction to British Culture, History of England, and Race in American Society. Unfortunately, there is no good statistical overview of this "culture" component within English studies. As Martin Kayman remarks of the responses to the last major survey of European English departments, "the categories 'Literature' and 'Linguistics' appeared to be universally recognizable, at least in their broad senses," but "the same was not necessarily true of the other major disciplinary areas we identified, 'Culture/Civilisation/Cultural Studies.'"[41] What seems clear is that while many European English departments continue to highlight national "culture" or "civilization" as part of their curricular remit, it rarely amounts to much

Foundation Course			
Focus	**Course**	**ECTS***	**US†**
Semester 1			
Literature	Literature 1: Genres, Texts, Contexts	6	3
	Introduction to Literary Studies (Comp. Lit. Dep.)	9	5
	Academic Research and Writing: Literature/Culture	3	2
		18	10
Language	Language Acquisition 1: Translation and Grammar	6	3
	Linguistics 1: Language Variation and Change	6	3
		12	6
Semester 2			
Literature	Literature 2: Medieval & Early Modern	6	3
	Literature 3: Romantic & Victorian	6	3
		12	6
Language	LA 2: English for Academic Purposes	6	3
	Introduction to Linguistics (General Ling. Dep.)	9	5
	Academic Research and Writing: Linguistics	3	2
		18	10
Second Year			
Semester 1			
Literature	Literature 4: Literary & Cultural Theory	6	3
		6	3
Language	Linguistics 2: Discourse and Pragmatics	9	5
	LA 3: Rhetorics and Writing	3	2
		12	7
Elective		12	7
Semester 2			
Literature	Literature 5: Modern & Contemporary	6	3
	Big Book Seminar	6	3
		12	6

Figure 3.5 Curriculum for the BA in English literature and culture (2011 matriculants), University of Amsterdam, Netherlands.

Source: Department of Language and Literature, Faculty of Humanities, University of Amsterdam, 2011.

Language	Linguistics 3: Language in Society	6	3
		6	3
Elective within English		12	6
Third Year			
Semester 1			
Foundations of the Humanities		12	6
Elective		18	9
Semester 2			
BA Thesis	Students select Literature or Language themed workshop groups	18	9
Elective		12	6

* ECTS = European Credit Transfer System units
† US = equiv. US Credits (semester-hours)

Figure 3.5 (Continued).

in the way of actual credit hours. The student who majors in English at Amsterdam earns a BA in English literature and culture, but, as one faculty member explains, "This really means mostly literature with the odd cultural studies oriented course and many [literature] courses with cultural (and a few media) studies elements."[42]

France might seem to be an exception in this respect – and, with its large number of English majors, an important one. As Jean Kempf explains, the crucial disciplinary units in the French system are the "sections" defined and authorized by the Ministry of Education, and in the case of English studies, the field has been configured as a cross-disciplinary section on the model of "area studies":[43]

> While many sections cover traditional "disciplines" in the scholarly sense of the term (history, sociology, philosophy, etc.), modern languages each belong to a specific section (German, English, Spanish, etc.) making them not disciplinary sections but area sections. So that a professor of American literature will not "belong" to a broad literature section but to an English-speaking world studies

147

section comprising specialists of literature, linguistics and the social sciences.

But this set-up affects faculty (whose hiring and promotion are overseen by their section) far more than it does students, who, at least at the baccalaureate level, are normally kept on a rather narrow path of literature and language courses through the multi-disciplinary English unit. They do take some classes such as American Society or English Civilization, but as often as not these are taught by literature specialists – who continue to dominate the modern language sections – rather than historians or social scientists. And while "culture" courses of this kind would form a greater part of the curriculum in France than in Italy, Spain, or the countries of Eastern Europe, French English departments have been more resistant than departments in most countries to other kinds of culture study, tending to offer fewer options in media, music, popular entertainment, and subculture studies. While the French area studies model might seem to lend itself to post-disciplinary sociological approaches to culture along the lines established at Birmingham, this has not been the case. As Kempf remarks, "Popular culture as an academic field is virtually nonexistent in France."[44]

Not that classes explicitly framed as "cultural studies" rather than literary studies are very numerous in any of Europe's English departments. The curriculum as described at Amsterdam – where there are few courses in cultural studies as such but "many with cultural (and a few media) studies elements" – is about as far in this direction as the European English studies faculties tend to go. A single advanced elective in cultural theory and a few others in, for example, Modernism and Jazz or Literature and Other Media (seminars offered at Basel) seem to be the norm within English BA programs. Even these classes tend to be literary in their orientation. Literature and Other Media, for example, is essentially a seminar in the recent history of the book, with readings drawn from American experimental authors like Robert Coover and Tom Philips as well as from the McSweeney's family of print, DVD, and web literature.[45] Where full-blown programs in cultural studies are found at all, they tend to be at the MA level, and are usually offered under auspices separate from the English Department.[46]

Nor are things radically different from this in the American universities. The cultural studies paradigm figured menacingly in the crisis narratives of the late 1980s and early 1990s; it was tagged as the enemy of literature within literature departments themselves, a rapidly expanding threat to our discipline's future. But 20 years on, cultural studies seems if anything less prominent in the curriculum now than it was then. The melding of literary studies, Western Marxist theory, and the sociology of everyday culture into a new hybrid project of research and pedagogy appears to have foundered at the gulf between qualitative and quantitative methods, with the sociologists going one way and literary scholars going the other.[47] Antony Easthope could expect widespread assent when he observed in 1991 that English literary studies had had its day and was now "being transformed into something else, Cultural Studies."[48] But surveying the past two decades one can see that not only in the countries of its most dramatic expansion but even in the United Kingdom and the United States, English studies has for the most part hugged close to the traditional objects of its attention – novels, plays, and poems. It has fostered expansion of the literary canon in terms of the social identities of authors deemed worthy of attention (with nearly all US English departments now offering numerous courses in African American, Asian American, and Gay and Lesbian literature, as well as far more extensive choices in women's literature than 30 years ago), but the canon has not opened beyond a point to nonliterary forms. Such broadening of forms and media as has occurred over the last two decades has been more pronounced in the genres of written history – letters, diaries, memoirs, speeches, and contemporaneous nonfiction (medical and legal writings, etc.) – than in the "subliterary" forms so alarmingly evoked by defenders of the book: television commercials, music videos, pornographic magazines, and spectator sports.[49] The one graphic novel that has been widely taught by English faculty, *Maus* by Art Spiegelman,[50] is a decidedly literary instance of the form, at safe remove from the works favored by knowledgeable readers of the graphic novel. Even cinema, which, to be sure, has become a curricular staple in English departments, accounting for several courses on a typical English BA transcript, is commonly used as a way into the literary canon rather than out of it, with "adaptation" being a dominant course rubric (Shakespeare and Cinema, Adapting Austen, etc.), or films included as sweeteners in traditional genre- or theme-based novel classes (Romantic Comedy, War Narratives).

There is nothing inherently wrong with this conservatism, which in many respects has served the discipline well through the period of its global expansion. But it seems to me that if anything we have constrained our objects and methods of cultural inquiry too much rather than too little. What seems to have happened at most American (and British) universities is that the literary faculty, despite having helped to pioneer the field of media studies, has ceded the lion's share of that terrain to other programs and departments with which they have then been reluctant to collaborate: sociology, communications, and media arts. Given that reading books is a declining practice, especially among 18-24 year olds, it may be time to reconsider our discipline's stubborn accordance of privilege to the print medium.[51] Why do we continue to approach cinematic adaptation via the now largely irrelevant question of interpretative fidelity to a literary original?[52] Why do we continue to eschew the audiobook, a popular and rapidly evolving form of digital literature that is already well disseminated among both college students and faculty yet has no place whatsoever in our curriculum?[53] We have succeeded all too well in containing the "threat" posed by cultural studies, missing many opportunities to widen the discipline's aperture to new literary objects, new pedagogical strategies, and new, less tried-and-true forms of inter-disciplinarity – in particular, those that would open conversations with "the dreaded quantitative social sciences" and encourage our use of empirical methods.[54] The one great exception has been the field of book history, whose recent vibrancy is owing in part to its pioneering research into new media and in part to its embrace of large datasets, quantitative analysis, and innovative forms of visual presentation.[55] So far, however, this field has affected baccalaureate-level curricula and pedagogy only at the margins.

In any event, the point here is that for all their reputed emphasis on "culture and civilization," the European English departments have no more tilted their curriculum toward the study of nonliterary texts than have departments in the United Kingdom and the United States, with their supposed over-accommodation of the cultural studies agenda. Indeed, compared with the United States, where a typical English major might take two or three classes in film or film–lit adaptation, the "culture" component of the European English curriculum is on the small side. What we find consistently in Europe are substantial requirements in the received canon of British and American literature. As has always been the case through the whole history of the discipline at all sites of its dissemination, that canon creeps forward over time toward more contemporary works. This is how the process of canon formation traditionally works: English studies is born from the dropping of classics in favor of moderns, and has gradually dropped early moderns in favor of later ones, and modernists themselves in favor of post–modernists. And one effect of this traditional forward movement is that American literature and to a lesser extent postcolonial Anglophone literature are gradually claiming a larger piece of the curriculum. But the British component still remains significantly larger at nearly all the European universities in terms of both faculty strength and course offerings. The course syllabi are dominated by major authors, with Shakespeare a virtually universal requirement. As compared with the United States, where (much to the horror of cultural conservatives who misapprehend tradition as stasis) many programs have jettisoned the medieval component and large swaths of pre–1800 literature in order to accommodate the expanded canon of twentieth–century works,[56] the pace of the curricular creep toward the present appears to be far more moderate in Europe. Pre–twentieth–century literature still represents some 70% of the curriculum in a majority of departments.[57] Browsing the European course catalogs, what is most striking is the curricular conservatism of English studies throughout that region, its capacity to maintain a fairly stable set of core texts and methods through an extended period of social and institutional tumult.

There is another country, however, that presents itself as perhaps an even better candidate for statistical outlier where cultural studies is concerned: Australia. Australia began its impressive shift to mass higher education during the very period of cultural studies' ascendancy, the years between the mid-1960s and the mid-1980s. In the course of those two decades, enrollments grew by 900 percent. Major new universities were launched, among them Griffith, Murdoch, Macquarie, Latrobe, Newcastle, Flinders, and Wollongong. At these start-up institutions, the traditional disciplines could be configured in innovative ways without pushing against the inertia of existing faculty habituated to conventional divisions and boundaries of departmental turf. Add to this the generally positive attitude in the 1960s and 1970s toward educational experiment and progressive reform and it is no surprise that Australian universities – in particular the newer ones – have tended more than universities elsewhere toward nontraditional interdisciplinary clusters involving literary, media, musical, and visual studies.[58] These formations have continued to evolve over time, through some major rearrangements of the entire higher educational sector. But the upshot is that degree programs and departments in cultural studies, often involving faculty with backgrounds in literary study, are more common in Australia than elsewhere, while English itself is often bundled with other cultural forms in a cross-disciplinary academic unit that would seem odd in most other countries.[59] At Wollongong, to take one example, English Literature shares departmental space with two other fields, Philosophy and Science and Technology Studies, while the more conventional partner unit, English Language and Linguistics, is located in a separate school. Even at the oldest universities – those constituting the "Group of Eight" – English is now often part of an unusual disciplinary mash-up suggesting a cultural studies perspective. At the University of Sydney, for example, English is housed in the School of Letters, Arts, and Media (SLAM); and at

Queensland, in the School of English, Media Studies, and Art History (EMSAH).

The Australian system is, at the same time, characterized by a strong bias toward vocationalism. The country has no long tradition of popular support for higher education as a vehicle of personal and intellectual growth or as a means of advancing knowledge for its own sake. The case for expansion has always had to be made on the basis of direct links between college studies and professional careers or between academic research and the needs of government and industry. This vocational orientation was arguably reinforced more than it was tempered by the integration, in the late 1980s and early 1990s, of the former technical and vocational colleges (the state-run Colleges of Advanced Education, or CAEs) into the public university system. The move, undertaken around the same time England recast its polytechnics as the New Universities, represented a shift away from the two-tier vocational and higher educational model (though there is still a very large Technical and Further Education [TAFE] layer of the Australian tertiary system). But it also greatly expanded enrollments at the established universities in such fields as Engineering, Information Sciences, Education, and Social Work.[60] One effect of this integration of vocational fields into the traditional bastions of the humanities, and the concomitant imposition of a new, competitive funding model, has been to push some of the already interdisciplinary clusters of literary, media, and film studies toward the fields of arts management and cultural policy studies as well as toward the fields of fundable academic research (audience studies, studies of the media industries, and other areas of communications and sociology). Thus for example even at the University of Melbourne, which has denounced the prevailing climate of preprofessionalism and launched an unprecedentedly broad, liberal arts–style curriculum (the so-called Melbourne model), English is housed in the School of Culture and Communications alongside programs in Arts Management, Media and Communications, and Publishing and Communications.

From my perspective, this institutional support for interdisciplinary approaches to cultural study – especially for forms of interdisciplinarity that extend beyond the humanities – is an attractive feature of the Australian system. And there is no question that Australia has produced some of the most distinguished and influential scholars of cultural studies: Tony Bennett, John Frow, Graeme Turner, and Meaghan Morris, to name just a few who have helped to extend the field of English studies in new directions and to articulate its relationship to the sociology of culture. At the same time, with Australian higher education facing the familiar two-pronged attack of less government funding coupled with more government interference and control, it is clear that interdisciplinary configurations are these days being shaped less by the intellectual and pedagogical aims of progressive educators than by centrally contrived budgetary pressures and/or executive fiat. There is more real estate available for cultural studies in the Australian system than elsewhere – in fact, by official government count, there are more full-time employees (FTE)s in "cultural studies" than in "literary studies" – but the scholars working in those precincts are not enjoying much sense of institutional privilege or autonomy.[61]

For our purposes here, though, the question is how this comparatively accommodating environment for cultural studies has affected the discipline of English and especially its undergraduate curriculum. Once again, the answer appears to be "less than we might have expected." Nationwide, there are more students doing BA programs in the subject area of "communications and media studies" than in "language and literature," and, thanks to the overwhelming preference for the former among the fast-growing population of foreign (mostly East Asian) students, the gap is widening.[62] It is also the case that students doing literature degrees in Australia are likely to take significantly more classes in media, communications, and the arts than students elsewhere; their education is shaped by a disposition toward interdisciplinary and multimedia cultural studies. But when we focus on what English majors do specifically within the English major to fulfill their major requirements, we find that at most universities there is only modest deviation from the general Anglophone model.

The standard minimum requirement for a 3-year bachelor's degree in Australia is 144 units of credit (UOCs), or 4 classes per semester, 24 in all, with each class typically meeting 3 hours a week and counting as 6 UOCs. To earn a degree in English, students are generally required to take at least a third of those 24 classes in the discipline. At the University of Sydney, for example, English majors must complete 48 to 84 units of credit (between 8 and 13 classes) in English, with the rest spread among linguistics, digital culture, media and communications, performance studies, religious studies, and art history/film studies. A typical English major takes more than the required minimum of 8 English classes, though fewer than the permitted maximum. A few of those classes may be in a "related" cultural field, cross-listed in English from a different unit within SLAM, but at least 6 must be actually rostered by the English Department. And these are basically courses in British, American, or Australian literary studies. Of 36 classes offered to non-Honours BA students in 2011, 6 were in grammar, rhetoric, Old English, or Old Norse; 2 in film; 1 in film and literature (adaptation); 1 in literary theory; and the remaining 26 in literary studies, from "Studies in Medieval Literature" to "Shakespeare," "Australian Gothic," and "Contemporary British Fiction." If we count the courses in Old English and Old Norse (which are as much about the premodern literary canon as they are about language and linguistics), the course in literary theory (which treats our discipline's foundational question: what, rigorously defined, is the "literary"?), and the course in cinematic adaptations of the novel as legitimate classes in literary study, the department's course offerings are nearly 90% literary.

There are other departments in Australia whose curriculum inclines somewhat more toward cultural studies than this, but none in which the literary component has ceased to anchor the curriculum. At the University of Melbourne, the basic major requirements are a little looser than Sydney's; again between 8 and 14 courses must be taken in the major, but only 5 of those have to be chosen from the English literary studies offerings. The remaining classes may be drawn from a larger list that includes courses in "Hong

Kong Cinema," "From Rock to Rave," and "Sports, Entertainment, and the Media." But even this broader list of classes in related areas includes only 8 that might be labeled cultural studies courses, versus 28 in literary studies. The literature classes push the envelope of the received canon somewhat harder than at Sydney: there's a class in Aboriginal poetry, drama, and fiction, for example, as well as one called Genre Fiction/Popular Fiction that includes Jackie Collins's *The Stud*, and another entitled Medievalism in Contemporary Culture that includes *Shrek*, *Braveheart*, and the *Lord of the Rings* films. But the Medievalism students also read Malory's *La Morte d'Arthur*, Seamus Heaney's translation of *Beowulf*, and four or five novels; the Genre Fiction class includes Arthur Conan Doyle, H.G. Wells, and Agatha Christie; and one class in the nation's indigenous literature is scarcely a sign that the department has abandoned the classics. (Indeed, the more usual complaint is that Australia's English departments have abandoned the country's own authors and works in favor of works by "outsiders.")[63] A lot of the classes that sound most edgy and interdisciplinary are in fact entirely devoted to close study of literary works. In Art/Pornography/Blasphemy/Propaganda, for example, students read their way through a formidably high–literary syllabus that includes *The Picture of Dorian Gray*, *Lady Chatterley's Lover*, *A Day in the Life of Ivan Denisovich*, *The Unbearable Lightness of Being*, *The Story of O.*, *American Psycho*, and *The Satanic Verses*.

To be sure, these English programs, like the others in Australia, are untraditional in various ways. There are no national, period, or genre requirements, no mandatory class on Chaucer or Shakespeare. Students have considerable license to determine both how much of their undergraduate coursework they do in the major, and how much of that will be devoted to literary studies. An English major at Melbourne, or even at Sydney, could, if she chose very carefully, avoid taking more than one or two classes in literary studies, and in effect complete a major in cultural studies within the English department. But if she were mainly interested in nonliterary cultural study, other major programs would be more appealing and much simpler to negotiate than English, where the courses on offer are 75–90% literary. The more typical student would take mostly (75–90%) literature classes to fulfill the 8 required courses in the major, using the remaining 16 classes (some perhaps in fulfillment of a second major, and some probably still in English) to explore more widely. The Australian student who majors in English does often end up with an undergraduate education in "cultural studies," having taken a rich mix of classes in literature, digital media, film studies, performance studies, and communications. But she would typically have taken 6 to 8 classes (of the 8 to 14 in the major) that fall squarely in the field of literary studies – the equivalent, once again, of about 300-400 contact hours. As in the United Kingdom, there will also be a fraction of those students (about 10% nationwide in Australia) who continue on for a fourth, Honours year, completing another 3-4 courses as well as a thesis in literary studies. But the normal route to a baccalaureate in English would involve roughly the same amount of literary study as in the other countries we have been surveying.

Like our expected outlier with respect to the language component of the discipline, China, our two expected outliers with respect to the "culture" component of the curriculum – Europe, with its traditional emphasis on "language, literature, and culture," and Australia, with its standout strength in "cultural studies" – differ little from each other or from other countries when it comes to the quantity and content of literary studies required of an English major. The discipline's widely deplored abandonment of the literary classics for ephemeral works of popular entertainment and screen culture, no less than its dreaded devolution into remedial courses in the communication arts, turns out to be less fact than fiction.[64]

Creative Writing for a Creative Economy

To complete this brief global survey of the bachelor's curriculum in English studies, we need to consider one further component, which, though tiny in comparison with language studies and less present even than film and media studies in the English programs of more recently emergent higher educational systems, may yet prove to be the most consequential for our discipline's future: creative writing. In *The Program Era*, Mark McGurl has provided a scintillating and authoritative history of the creative writing program and its enormous impact not just on higher education but also on the whole field of literary production in the post-war United States.[65] The "program" on which McGurl focuses his analysis is the master's or more especially the MFA program, and he says little about the way creative writing has affected the discipline of English at the undergraduate level. This is understandable. The writer's workshop originated as a master's program, and the MFA has long been the presumptive first and terminal degree in the field.[66] As recently as 1998, MA and MFA programs in creative writing outnumbered BA major programs by nearly 20 to 1. Of the 55,000 bachelor's recipients in English in 2009, only about 2300, or less than 5%, emerged from designated subprograms in creative writing.[67] These are the figures for the United States; the numbers are smaller but similarly lopsided in favor of post-graduate programs in other Anglophone countries.

It would be a mistake, however, to conclude that creative writing is an insignificant part of the undergraduate curriculum. From 1998 to 2008, the growth of MFA programs in the United States, though pretty robust (from 83 to 148), was slower than in previous decades, and the number of MA programs stalled completely at about 145. But, as indicated in Figure 3.6, the number of BA and BFA major programs increased more than tenfold, from just 12 to 147 – on top of some 300 minor programs.[68] Even Iowa, the original Writers' Workshop and an exclusively post-graduate program for more than 70 years, finally capitulated to this trend and extended a wing into the undergraduate curriculum in 2008.

We have in effect entered a second era in the rise of the creative writing program, the first wave of expansion now repeating itself at the undergraduate level. To the extent that it may be considered a field of specialization within English studies (and this will require further discussion below), creative writing is still a

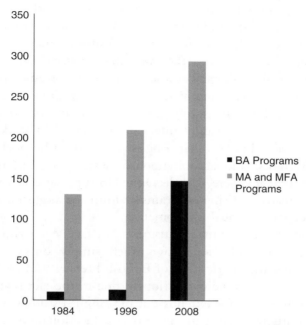

Figure 3.6 Number of programs awarding BAs and master's degrees in creative writing, 1984, 1996, and 2008.

Source: Association of Writers & Writing Programs, *AWP Official Guide to Creative Writing Programs.*

modest component of the curriculum in comparison with literary studies. But it has been dramatically outgrowing the rest of the discipline. This growth, moreover, is being fed by broader trends in higher education which show no signs of abating: toward more student-consumer choice; toward more double-major and individuated degree options; and toward the more creative and performative, practice-based fields within the arts and humanities.[69] And while the United States remains unsurpassed in the number and scale of its creative writing programs, the other Anglophone countries have been rapidly expanding in this area, too. Surveying the situation in Britain, Nick Everett observes that the growth in creative writing there, both "within and alongside English," has "accelerated markedly" since the mid-1990s.[70] In Australia, creative writing has been enjoying a tremendous boom, with an "extraordinary rise in student demand"; all 37 of the country's public universities now offer creative writing courses, a majority of them at baccalaureate level, and the Australian government ranks the discipline ahead of literary studies and cultural studies in overall quality and even in terms of its production of "research."[71] With the spread of English as the preferred medium of college-level instruction, the increasingly international traffic in students, and the rise of "new literatures in English" produced by poets, novelists, playwrights, and autobiographers writing in English as an adopted language, there is little reason to suppose that the proliferation of creative writing programs "within and alongside English" cannot become a global phenomenon.

But how much of this expansion is, in fact, occurring within, how much alongside, and how much simply outside or even actively *against* the curriculum of English literary studies? The difficulty in answering these questions is due to the fact that creative writing connects to (or extends out of) English studies from, as it were, two different zones in the tertiary educational system, which might be thought of as higher and lower than English itself. On the higher side are the fine arts workshops described by McGurl, which are essentially elite programs for budding poets or writers of literary fiction. These programs make a special, highly desirable space within the humanities for the gifted young literary genius or self-declared free spirit. Such programs, as McGurl remarks, seem even less practical, more privileged, and more self-indulgent than even a supposedly rarified field like English: they serve as soft shelters where "the student is validated as a creative person and given temporary cover, by virtue of his student status, from the classic complaint of middle-class parents that their would-be artist children are being frivolous" (17). This view of creative writing is prevalent in the United States, where the ostensive "first-ever" creative writing course was taught by a professor of English, Barrett Wendell, at our most elite university, Harvard, as an early experiment in progressive education designed to free the young English major from set topics and exam questions and let him write on what truly ignited his passions.[72] The conventional curriculum of literary study was seen by bold reformers like Wendell as stifling higher forms of creative talent that could only be captured by a more advanced pedagogical framework. Emerging from this lofty agenda, the MFA programs have become by some measures the apex of the entire education system. Accepting just one or two applicants out of every hundred, they are the most selective degree programs in the world, more so even than the professional programs at Yale Law School, Harvard Medical School, and Stanford Graduate School of Business, or any of the leading PhD programs.[73]

The astonishing selectivity of even the middling American MFA programs enables them to "validate" students' literary creativity by marking it as *rare*, a special giftedness, recognized by the literary masters or genius figures who preside over the workshop and who personally select the favored few. The programs' selectivity has contributed to the growth of creative writing at the undergraduate level, which serves in part to groom students for success in the ever more daunting MFA application process. But the growth has also been driven simply by demand among undergraduates for a corresponding space of validation within the baccalaureate program – a demand that runs especially strong at the more competitive colleges, whose own ever-increasing selectivity has already marked their students as exceptional, gifted, and so on. Indeed, many of the undergraduate creative writing programs are themselves internally selective in a way that differentiates them from all the other tracks available to English majors. To concentrate in creative writing at the University of North Carolina at Chapel Hill (UNC Chapel Hill), for example, a student must be nominated by a faculty member; at University of California, Santa Cruz (UC Santa Cruz), students must meet a threshold GPA and submit work judged promising of literary talent. As their program website proudly declares, "Students in the creative writing concentration [represent] . . . a disproportionate number of honors and high honors students in the [literature] department." Indeed, given the special selection process, creative writing tracks of this kind are less like the other concentrations than like honors programs in their own right.

Even these programs that emphasize their selectivity and restrictiveness have been growing rapidly to accommodate increased student demand, and those which impose no special hurdles to admission are growing more rapidly still. In my own department at Penn, creative writing was first introduced as a concentration in 1999 and quickly became the most popular option; today it claims a third of all our majors. If some of these creative writing concentrators are the kind of English majors who "don't like to read," others are among our most avid student-scholars. And the reading-averse students cannot escape literary studies by choosing the creative writing option. On the contrary, these sorts of programs (i.e., special tracks within English for aspiring "literary" writers) tend to emphasize critical reading in their mission statements and to build all the standard core requirements of the English major into their curriculum. Penn's department is fairly typical in that the creative writing concentrators are required to take the normal six courses in literary study (distributed in specific ways across genres, nationalities, and historical periods) plus two advanced literary seminars, topping off this standard curriculum with at least three creative writing seminars. The ratio of (literary) core to (creative) concentration is thus 8:3 or 8:4, depending on what is chosen for the elective twelfth class. Similar ratios of core to concentration, and of reading courses to writing courses, are found at most undergraduate English and creative writing programs in the United States and many in the United Kingdom: between 10:3 and 8:5 at Colorado State, 8:5 at Loyola University of Chicago and UNC Chapel Hill, 9:3 at East Anglia, 8:4 at Nottingham, and so on.[74] There are a few programs, such as those at Carnegie Mellon and at UC Santa Cruz, where the number of required writing courses is as high as 6 out of 12, but these are rare. Given that the workshop model of pedagogy depends on small class size, only the largest, best-funded, and most selective programs can staff enough writing classes for this kind of a curriculum to be practicable. Programs with as modest a literary requirement as this tend also to be free-standing bachelor's degree programs, where students receive a BA in creative writing rather than a BA in English and creative writing or a BA in English with emphasis in creative writing. Such free-standing programs (which are still quite rare) might be seen as compromising the literature curriculum – except for the fact that they usually make a double-major with English almost irresistible. At Carnegie Mellon, for example, just three additional literature classes puts a bachelor of arts in English on the transcript. Students who take this popular route end up with just as many courses in literary studies as non-creative writing concentrators.

We should keep in mind that courses that satisfy the core requirements in English are more canonically literary in their orientation than is the curriculum as a whole. The core courses tend toward period surveys, major author classes (especially Shakespeare), and introductions to national or ethnic literatures. Insofar as there is an internal trade-off for English studies between creative writing and other subfields, it tends to affect enrollments at the less literary, more heterogeneous end of the curriculum: the classes in film studies, detective fiction, art books, and so on. The upshot is that students in these creative writing programs in the United States are mostly completing at least 300 classroom hours of traditional literary study. As they represent a minority of English majors even at the institutions where creative writing is a well-established field, and a much smaller minority of all US English majors (most of whom take no creative writing workshops as such), their numbers do not at this point alter our rough estimate of 400 classroom hours of literary study for US English majors. About 1800 total hours (120 semester hours) are generally required for the bachelor's degree, of which 600–650 are typically required as a minimum in the major (but 700–800 actually taken, since students lean toward their own major subjects in choosing free electives). The breakdown for average figures in the English major would thus be approximately 50 classroom hours in language skills and composition; 150 in film, media, or other cultural study; 100 in creative writing; 400 in literature; and 1000–1100 in other subjects, including college-wide requirements as well as a second major and/or a minor.[75]

Considered in this light, the rise of creative writing seems a benign and even a welcome development for English studies. While some students in the discipline end up doing more writing and less reading than traditional English majors, there is clearly a widespread pedagogical commitment to maintaining the connection between the two. Indeed, judging from published reflections on the state of their field as well as from the descriptive and promotional language they have crafted for program websites, creative writing faculty are more committed to the literary canon (if not always to the contemporary forms of its study) than are English faculty who specialize in film or cultural studies. And who's to say that English departments are bleeding more students from their literary curriculum into creative writing than creative writing is luring into the English major in the first place?

But this is to consider creative writing only in the forms it has taken within and "above" English, as a special zone of fine-artistic license for humanities students, configured in ways that have tended to assure its close proximity to the English faculty and its curricular commitment to the academic subject of literary studies. As I remarked at the outset, there is another and equally important form of creative writing that we might think of as emerging within and "below" English studies. That same class taught by Barrett Wendell at Harvard, frequently invoked as the first university course in creative writing, is also widely cited as a pedagogical watershed in the low-status zone of composition instruction.[76] If we turn from the elite fine-arts workshops with their revered masters and gifted acolytes, we can see links between creative writing and the strictly vocational field of professional writing, a field that appears from the vantage of English studies as embarrassingly practical and job oriented, a kind of extended certification program in written communication, where future content drones acquire transportable composition skills.

In the United Kingdom and Australia, creative writing began for the most part in this vocational mode, on the lower rungs of the tertiary system such as the polytechnics and colleges of education; it provided practical training and guidance to future trade journalists, technical writers, primary school teachers, corporate communications personnel, and media industry workers. Even now in Britain, the elite universities, with the most highly regarded English departments, are the least likely to house an undergraduate degree program in creative writing or to offer a creative writing track for English majors. At Oxford and Cambridge, the subject is available at the undergraduate level only to part-time students in continuing education. At the University of Edinburgh, there is a one-year MSc program but nothing for undergraduates. At University College London, there is no creative writing curriculum at any level. In contrast, at former polytechnics such as the University of East London, London South Bank, and London Metropolitan, there are full-scale bachelor's degree programs offering the BA (Hons) in creative writing either as a single degree or as joint-honours with another discipline.

Of course, creative writing, whether it conforms to the higher educational fine arts model or the lower post-secondary job-training model, is inherently vocational in a way that literary studies is not. Most students see the kinds of writing they do in their creative writing workshops as a version of what they would hope to be doing in their careers; their degree program has them practicing what they envision themselves doing after graduation. One can hardly say the same of English majors, only a tiny fraction of whom (those bound for PhD programs) would imagine themselves continuing to generate critical essays and exam papers once they leave college. English has billed itself, at least since the interventions of F. R. Leavis in the 1930s and 1940s, as a discipline that offers preparation for lives of discerning and critical leadership in the community, quite the opposite in fact of training for a salaried position as a producer of text in the corporate cubicle. Considered from this standpoint, the dramatic rise of creative writing at the undergraduate level starts to look like yet another symptom of the decline of English studies, its slide from a uniquely privileged position as both the most central and the most elevated discipline of the modern university, the educational base for a vital project of social renovation and collective moral improvement,[77] toward the basement-level service work of Communications 101, vocational training in "corporate communication skills."

It would be hard not to notice that the growth in college programs that produce certified "creative writers" has coincided more or less exactly with the growth of what Richard Caves has termed the "Creative Industries" and the concomitant expansion of the workforce in those industries.[78] Richard Florida has described the members of that workforce as a kind of new working class, a "creative class" which has surpassed the traditional working class in both population and economic importance in the most advanced societies.[79] Much of what the United States and the United Kingdom manufacture in their post-industrial phase is "creative" content for the global media corporations. These behemoths, comprising literally thousands of subsidiary units, need "creative" workers capable of writing, editing, and just plain churning out massive quantities of text. And lo and behold, there's a boom in undergraduate "creative writing" programs. Rather than rejoice at the sudden vibrancy of one of our traditional subfields, should we not suspect its co-optation by newly euphemized forms of professional writing? Is the seeming stampede of BA students into creative writing less a matter of their desire to approach literature from the perspective of a budding artist than of their practical desire for training as laborers in the new "creative" working class?

It is perhaps invidious to make a distinction between "true" writing workshops that nurture literary talent and artistic ambitions, and "mere" composition classes that impart the basic knowledge and skills needed to get a job in the creative wings of the culture industry. Those in the less privileged tiers of academe may harbor high ambitions, and those in the most selective workshops are scarcely indifferent to their career prospects. But the way this distinction plays out institutionally, in terms of academic divisions and disciplines, has real consequences for English studies. Essentially, the more a creative writing program tilts toward the vocational, the less its curriculum overlaps with core requirements in English; the less likely its students are to major, double-major, or minor in

English; and the less its faculty will have to do with the concerns of the English department. Depending on its institutional position and orientation, creative writing either complements and supports the discipline of English, maintaining what for English studies must always be a bedrock pedagogical principle, namely, that the ability to write creatively develops in tandem with the ability to read critically; or it marginalizes the discipline of English and directly undermines its pedagogy, proposing to teach all the skills needed to write for the creative industries without developing any skills of critical reading, and indeed without imparting any knowledge of literature as an academic subject. Creative writing either emphasizes the continuing importance of literary skills and values in the evolving media sphere – the relevance, let's say, of Shakespeare to screenwriting – or it treats the literary as an anachronism and an irrelevance for the creators of today's media content. These are not negligible stakes.

If what is occurring today were simply the growth of two entirely different and separate kinds of academic program, we would have little cause for concern. At one end of the university we would find creative writing, a field in the arts and humanities historically interwoven with English literary studies and becoming more popular as a major, a minor, or a special and often selective track in English for the bachelor of arts degree. At the other end we would find professional writing, a field in communications, education, and media arts historically disconnected from English literary studies and, with the rise of the so-called creative industries, becoming more popular as a subject for vocational certificates and bachelors of science degrees. There are indeed universities that offer degree programs in both fields, through widely separated wings of the faculty. At Northwestern, for example, there is a creative writing concentration within the English Department in the College of Arts and Sciences. Admission to the program is competitive, and students who are admitted must satisfy English major requirements and take at least six "pure literature" classes ("courses in which the bulk of the reading is literature") at the advanced, 300-level. But there is also a separate program in creative writing for the media, a nonselective track for students pursuing the bachelor of science degree in the Radio/Television/Film Department of Northwestern's School of Communications. This program has no literary studies component. Similarly, at the University of Nottingham in the United Kingdom there is a BA (Hons) program in English with creative writing, offered through the School of English Studies. It is a selective program, and consists of two-thirds literary studies and one-third creative writing. For students in Nottingham's School of Education, there is a BA (Hons) program in creative and professional writing, a nonselective program with, again, no required coursework in literary studies. The traditional status-and-privilege gap is signaled in the School of Education's FAQ, which, by way of answering the prospective student's question about how to choose between these two programs in "creative writing," observes that "the School of English, one of the oldest schools in the University, is noted for its academic excellence," while the School of Education's program "attracts students of very varied ages and backgrounds."

Yet even at these universities, a certain slipperiness is evident around the term (never a very satisfactory one) "creative." Where we would once have expected simply "professional writing," we increasingly find such formulations as Northwestern's Creative Writing for the Media or Nottingham's Creative and Professional Writing. The latter label is now being used at a number of institutions in the United Kingdom, for example at Bangor University in Wales, where students can also pursue a BA in creative writing and media. In Australia, too, there are programs in creative and professional writing, as for example at Queensland University of Technology, where that degree is offered by the Faculty of Creative Industries. A similar program at the University of South Australia is called Writing and Creative Communication. There are also professional writing programs that retain the traditional name, but are now offering a concentration in creative writing, following the model of English studies ("with Emphasis in Creative Writing") while diverging entirely from the English curriculum. An example is Western Connecticut State University, where the only creative writing program available to students is the creative writing concentration in professional writing offered by the Department of Writing, Linguistics, and the Creative Process.

This terminological slippage, with "creative" functioning as a kind of relay between two previously more distinct zones of the tertiary system, is helping to open an ambiguous space for creative writing somewhere between the humanities and the professional schools, where the relationship to English is indeterminate. An example is the Creative Writing and Publishing Department at Bath Spa University, a former College of Education in the United Kingdom. This well-regarded department has a clear vocational stance, encouraging students "from the start . . . to orient themselves to the world of the creative industries," and offering them "opportunities to work with industry professionals." The language of creative industries and creative media is everywhere in their catalog and promotional materials. But the department is housed in a hybrid School of Humanities and Cultural Industries, which also contains the Department of English Literature. The BA curriculum is loose, with a wide range of options, but the program makes some effort to "combine the . . . the practice of writing with the study of exemplary authors." The Creative Writing and English Literature faculties have 17 members between them with 7 exclusive to English Literature, 6 exclusive to Creative Writing, and 4 holding joint appointments and teaching modules in both. This is far more overlap than exists between Creative Writing and any of the other departments in the school, and would seem to encourage students to choose their elective modules in English, since many of those modules would be staffed by their own faculty. And while it appears that single Honours degrees are the norm, the joint degree with English is a prominent option.[80]

From the vantage point of English studies, programs like this represent a threat but also an opportunity: a threat inasmuch as they show how a highly rated program in creative writing, with a faculty that leans toward literary fiction and poetry and includes writers shortlisted for the Booker Prize and the T.S. Eliot Prize, may establish itself as an academic unit independent of English and largely concerted around a vocational understanding of creativity – the "creativity" of the creative industries. The growth of creative writing programs, even as academic units within English, affords those units more autonomy, such that the BA in English with emphasis on creative writing morphs over time into the BA in creative writing (with or without a concentration in English) and the Creative Writing Program becomes the Department of Creative Writing. With autonomy comes a new freedom of choice as regards institutional and intellectual alliances. And as this process unfolds, English could be a huge loser. Creative writing could go the way of rhetoric and composition, institutionally decoupling from English and advancing a pedagogy implicitly or explicitly hostile to that of literary studies.

But programs like those at Bath Spa also represent an opportunity. The surge of students into programs of creative writing, and the resultant growth and reconfiguration of these programs, could bring a new generation of undergraduates with broadly literary ambitions into curricular contact with English. As I suggested above, students choosing programs in Writing for the Creative Industries may have literary aspirations no less intense than those of students in the most selective English with Emphasis in Creative Writing tracks, and they may be drawn to writing by the same desires for self-expression and validation of their creativity. To be sure, an expanding market for creative-class workers will tend to redirect students into degree programs aligned with that market. But much nonsense in the higher education debates arises from an assumption that more freedom for students to choose their curriculum means a shift toward more vocational fields, that students' choices of major subjects are mainly guided by practical and mercenary considerations. If students flocked straight to the fields where jobs are plentiful and salaries high, we would not have such a shortage of engineering majors or such dramatic growth in religious studies (or, for that matter, in creative writing). Many students will choose a reputedly less practical field that they find congenial and exciting over a reputedly more practical one that they see as dreary or tedious. And they are right to do so, since they will develop more of the kind of basic analytical and problem-solving skills that employers actually want by engaging intensely with an "impractical" subject than by passively completing the major requirements in a "practical" one. This has been an important factor in English's long run as the largest discipline in the humanities; despite the decline of book reading as a practice among young people, English classes continue to offer a content as well as a pedagogical model possessing strong appeal. Creative writing may – and, I am arguing, not for merely practical and vocational reasons – have an appeal just as broad. What is evident at a program like Bath Spa is that, while English cannot claim ownership of creative writing, it is the academic subject most proximate to creative writing intellectually and institutionally and the one that is already most interwoven with its curriculum and most similar in its pedagogy. As universities tilt their programs in professional writing away from the old corporate composition curriculum toward the curriculum of creative-industry writing, they will be recruiting faculty more inclined to share our discipline's pedagogical stance regarding the inseparability of writing from reading and the necessity of supplementing the lessons learned in writing workshops with lessons learned from great authors of the past and present. It is not only poets, dramatists, and novelists who hold this view but writers for the screen media, too, if they are any good. Asked recently where he learned to write for television, what form of training or professional mentorship enabled him to forge his remarkable career (as a writer, creator, and producer of *Hill Street Blues, NYPD Blue,* and *Deadwood,* among other shows), David Milch dismissed the suggestion that he had learned anything important from TV itself or from his first TV boss, Steven Bochco. He learned to write, he said, in his literature classes at Yale, where he studied with the heavyweights of close reading Cleanth Brooks and Robert Penn Warren, and in his writing workshops at Iowa where (in 1969) students were not at all encouraged to "orient themselves to the world of the creative industries."[81]

Joining with our natural allies in creative writing to press this point about English and what it teaches is, for the time being, an agenda only for those of us who work in the Anglophone sphere. But it doesn't take much of a speculative leap to imagine the same combination of forces in other countries – the creative industries driving up the market for competent local producers of Anglophone content, and students demanding more curricular license to self-expression – pushing the foreign-language-and-literature paradigm of English studies toward something more like a foreign-language-and-creative-writing one. Since programs in these countries will likely take their cues from the Anglophone universities, there is all the more incentive for us to be vigilant and active, establishing clearer lines of communication not only with colleagues who teach the writing workshops but also with students who are drawn to creative writing. We do our students and ourselves a disservice if we imply that "creative" writing leaves off where literary studies begins. To approach a story or a play from the standpoint of an author can indeed be more enabling for an undergraduate than to approach it from the standpoint of a historian, sociologist, or psychoanalyst. Creative assignments in literature classes (e.g., imitation or parody of a classic work) are a proven way to engage students with a text, sharpening their reading skills and helping them see the essential connection between reading well and writing well. Creative writers know that even just the literal copying of favorite passages, word by word and line by line, can be a valuable exercise, forcing attention on how the sentences are constructed, how the dialogue is punctuated, how the characters are moved about, and so forth.[82] If English is to emerge from the undergraduate program era in a strengthened rather than weakened position, it needs to encourage traffic between the curricula of reading and of writing and to embrace the creative impulse, the impulse to artistic self-expression, as a fundamental aspect of literary study itself.

The Global English Major

Figure 3.7 attempts a graphic rendering of this very partial survey of the English major in different countries and regions around the

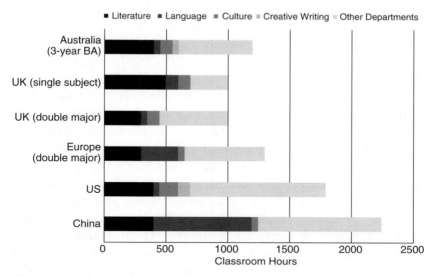

Figure 3.7 Approximate average distribution of classroom hours for an English BA in selected systems.

world. As we have seen, the complexion of the bachelor's degree programs as a whole — the total number of courses and contact hours, the amount of time spent on foreign language learning, the proportion of film and media studies versus introductory surveys in the other disciplines of the liberal arts, and so on — varies widely.[83] If you were looking at the transcripts of random English majors from Beijing, Lyon, Adelaide, and Miami, you would find them diverging in many respects. But if all the contents of those transcripts were blacked out except for the classes in English literary studies, you would be hard pressed to distinguish one from the next. If for English BA candidates in the United Kingdom we take the average of the single and the double majors, they are typically devoting about 400 hours of class time to the study of literary works, mostly works that we might find on course syllabi in any of the other countries we've been discussing. And while the typical English major in Europe (where single degrees are far rarer) might complete only 300 hours of literary study, that is the most significant variance we will find. Australia, China, and the United States all fall close to the 400 standard, as do South Africa, Canada, and India, which, though not pictured on this chart, are essentially mixtures of the UK and European regional paradigms.

Of course, the specific texts that students read will vary from term to term and from instructor to instructor even within a single course in a single department; there is no guarantee that two given English majors will both have read *Beloved* or even *Hamlet*. But it is almost certain that they will have read some Shakespeare and some contemporary American fiction, wherever they took their degrees and whatever their tracks or emphases. The newer, more "foreign" programs emerging with globalization are if anything more committed to the familiar canon of Great Authors than are the established programs of the Anglophone sphere, just as they are more traditionally formalist in their critical approach. Rather than pulling the discipline apart, the process of global massification is affirming its cohesion around a common core. It is time to stop fretting over the imagined disappearance of literature from literary studies and start considering how an essentially stable and healthy discipline, its tendencies toward innovation and interdisciplinarity tempered but not negated by its inherent conservatism, can best take advantage of its new global circumstances.

Notes

1. Average earnings of faculty, including full-time non-tenure track instructors, at degree-granting institutions place them in the top quintile in most countries, including the United States, where the cut-off for the 80th percentile in personal income was $57,000 in 2009 according to US Census Bureau statistics. That is about $4,000 below the average salary of faculty in English (one of the lowest paid academic fields), according to the annual survey of the College and University Professional Association for Human Resources. See Jill Laster, "One-Third of Faculty Members See Dip in Their Salaries," *Chronicle of Higher Education*, 8 March 2010.

2. On the size of the financial industry, from 1860 to the present, see the working paper of Thomas Philippon, "The Evolution of the US Financial Industry from 1860 to 2007," November 2008, http://pages.stern.nyu.edu/~tphilipp/papers/finsize.pdf. On the total public and private expenditure on education in the United States, see the Congressional Budget Office, *Issues and Options in Infrastructure Investment* (Washington: CBO, 2008), Appendix A: "Spending for Research and Development and for Education," Figure A-1: "U.S. R&D Spending as a Percentage of GDP, 1953 to 2006."

3. Andrew Sum *et al.*, "The 'Jobless and Wageless' Recovery from the Great Recession of 2007–2009: The Magnitude and Sources of Economic Growth through 2011 I and Their Impacts on Workers, Profits, and Stock Values," May (Boston: Northeastern University Center for Labor Market Studies, 2011).

4. Karen MacGregor sites Higher Education South Africa (HESA) data showing an increase from 473,000 in 1993 to 784,000 in 2008, to a projected 837,000 in 2011. Karen MacGregor, "State Funds for Student Expansion," *University World News* 23 (22 February 2009), http://www.universityworldnews.com/article.php?story=20090220072000658.

5. I am referring to the students classified as "African" in the Higher Education South Africa (HESA) data. These enrollments are continuing to climb at four times the rate of white enrollments, which by 2007 had fallen to 24% of the total, versus 63% African. See HESA, *Pathways to a Diverse and Effective South African Higher Education System: Strategic Framework 2010/2020*, Strategic Framework Booklet (Johannesburg: HESA, 2010), 2, 11, http://hedbib.iau-aiu.net/pdf/Pathways%20to%20a%20diverse%20and%20effective%20SA%20HE%20system.pdf.

6. Prescribed texts for these courses vary slightly from year to year; I am working from the 2011–2012 syllabi.

7. Since the economic crisis of 2007–2009 such programs have been cut back drastically in the United States, but the overall trend – quite pronounced in China and India – is for in-house corporate education programs to represent a growing fraction of overall educational expenditures.

8. A recent statistically driven study of US college students offers a mixed perspective on this question. According to Richard Arum

and Josipa Roksa in *Academically Adrift: Limited Learning on College Campuses* (Chicago: Chicago University Press, 2011), after 4 years in college, more than a third of all students have realized no significant improvement in "general analytical competencies" such as problem solving, persuasive writing, and critical thinking. For opponents of mass higher education, these are students who would be far better served by vocational training or workplace apprenticeship than they are by the college track. But Arum and Roksa's data also show that students majoring in the liberal arts realize "significantly higher gains" in "critical thinking, complex reasoning, and writing" during their years in college than do students majoring in other fields, particularly the vocational fields of business and education (104–106). Adjusting the data for students' social background and educational preparation and for the selectivity of the institution they attend reduces this gap, but the difference remains significant ("Methodological Appendix," Table 4.3). These findings would suggest that our tertiary system needs to be less, not more, vocationally oriented, and that the liberal arts education remains our best model for improving broadly analytical skills.

9. For an excellent overview of the new model and its implications, see Margaret Simons, "Dangerous Precedent: The Melbourne Model," *The Monthly* (March 2010): 32–39.

10. Committee to Advise on Renovation and Rejuvenation of Higher Education in India, "Renovation and Rejuvenation of Universities," 1 March 2009, http://www.academics-india.com/Yashpal-committee-report.pdf.

11. DUT was created by the merger in 2002 of Technikon Natal and M.L. Sultan Technikon and was known in its early years as Durban Institute of Technology. While DUT is still focused on vocational education, and its English track emphasizes communications rather than literature, it has significantly expanded its Faculty of Arts.

12. "It is becoming clear that a new version of English teaching has appeared on the scene, rapidly colonizing and indeed effectively commanding it. I shall call this 'English-as-Literacy', with a deliberate nod to the more familiar classificatory notions of 'English-as-Literature' and 'English-as-Language' – the so-called 'Cambridge' and 'London' Schools respectively." Bill Green, "Curriculum, 'English' and Cultural Studies; or Changing the Scene of English teaching?" *Changing English* 11.2 (2004): 297.

13. Such a comparative analysis is offered by contributors to "Law, Literature, and Language," a special issue of *European Journal of American Studies* 11.1 (2007).

14. As will become clear further on, I am greatly understating here the wide variability of English curricula and degree programs in Europe. The most comprehensive survey of English studies across Europe concludes that, as I have been indicating, "Literature and Linguistics [are] the two major parallel disciplinary areas, and [European English departments] have divided their requirements more or less evenly between the two" (see Martin A. Kayman, *Report on a Survey of English Studies in Europe* [Rome: European Society for the Study of English and the British Council, 2002], 7). But Kayman's survey also details many differences involving more or less emphasis on linguistics, various ways of coordinating dual-discipline degrees (which represent about three quarters of all English degree takers), and tracks or sections in "culture, civilization, or cultural studies" (more or less distinct from literature) and "English as a foreign language" (more or less distinct from linguistics).

15. ADE Ad Hoc Committee on the English Major, "The Undergraduate English Major," 183.

16. Kayman, *Report on a Survey on English Studies in Europe*, 6.

17. Of course, the demand for schoolteachers has declined in some countries, despite the worldwide trend. Spain and Portugal experienced sharp contractions in the hiring of new teachers beginning in the late 1990s.

18. 69% of English majors in the United States are women, 70% in the United Kingdom, and more than 75% in virtually all the countries of Europe. See Modern Language Association, *MLA Report to the Teagle Foundation*, http://www.mla.org/teaglereport_page, 22, Table 1; HESA, *Statistical First Release 153*, Table 7: "Qualifications Obtained by Students on HE Courses at HEIs in the United Kingdom by Level of Qualification Obtained, Gender and Subject Area 2005/06 to 2009/10"; and Kayman, *Report on a Survey of English Studies in Europe*, 12. A close look at the gender breakdown of a recent NCES *Digest of Education Statistics* from the US Department of Education shows the percentage of male English majors gradually rising over the last decade or so in the United States, possibly owing to the growth of creative writing, a subfield

177

in which males, though still outnumbered by females, are over-represented compared with the major as a whole.

19. MLA, *MLA Report to the Teagle Foundation*, 30. According to the taxonomic scheme used in this report, even at just 15%, the fraction of English BAs who go on to teach primary or secondary school is larger than the fraction pursuing any other career path. But there is other work on the post-collegiate lives of English majors that highlights a clear tendency away from teaching careers, stressing for example the much higher percentage of majors (30%) who go on to careers in business, industry, or law if those categories are combined. See for example Peter G. Beidler, "What English Majors Do Out There, How They Feel about It, and What We Do about It," *ADE Bulletin* 133 (Winter 2003): 29–35; and Kevin Brown, "What Can They Do with an English Major? Showing Students the Breadth of the Discipline," *CEA Forum* 38.2 (2009): http://www2.widener.edu/~cea/382brown.htm.

20. Braj B. Kachru, "Standards, Codification, and Sociolinguistic Realism: The English Language in the Outer Circle," in *English in the World: Teaching and Learning the Language and Literatures*, eds. Randolph Quirk and H.G. Widdowson (Cambridge: Cambridge University Press, 1985), 11–30.

21. On the separation of the two disciplines in Canada, see Anne Furlong, "A Modest Proposal: Linguistics and Literary Studies," *La Revue canadienne de linguistique appliquée* 10.3 (2007): 325–347.

22. Of 51 UK English departments surveyed by the English Subject Centre in 2003, all offered programs in literary studies, 21 (or about 40%) offered integrated programs of literary and language studies, and 8 (15%) offered a separate language studies track. Halcrow Group, Ltd., *Survey of the English Curriculum and Teaching in UK Higher Education*, LTSN English Subject Centre Report Series 8, October (Egham, UK: LTSN English Subject Centre, 2003).

23. Halcrow Group, *Survey of the English Curriculum*.

24. NCES, *Digest of Education Statistics* 2010, Table 286: "Bachelor's, Master's, and Doctor's Degrees Conferred by Degree-Granting Institutions, by Sex of Student and Discipline Division: 2008–09."

25. Statistics are given on the BA Program page of the department's website at http://www.tsinghua.edu.cn/publish/fdlen/1458. I have

adjusted these to reflect information gleaned from Weimin Zhang, associate professor in the department, when we met in June 2010.

26. For a clear if somewhat out-of-date appraisal of the ELT burden and its advantages as well as disadvantages for English as an academic subject, see Cheng Zhaoxiang, "English Departments in Chinese Universities: Purpose and Function," *World Englishes* 21 (2002): 257–267.

27. Similar enrollment statistics, reflecting the outsized service role of English departments in China, are observed at Sun Yat-Sen University in Guangzhou. There, the School of Foreign Languages, the largest program within which is English language and literature, has 47 full-time tenure-stream faculty and 2300 students. That's a very large number compared with, say, the History Department, which has 42 tenure-stream faculty but only 366 students. Looking closer, though, we see that of the 2300 students in the School of Foreign Languages, only 700 are classified as "undergraduates" (and another 180 as graduate students). That is still more than in History, but a BA program that graduates four students per tenure-stream faculty member each year is not grossly understaffed. As for the remaining 1400 students, listed as "other," these are presumably students from outside the School of Foreign Languages, taking basic language classes to improve their skills in English.

28. Huazhong Normal does not appear on any of the major rankings of top-100 Asian or top-1000 world universities such as those compiled by QS World University Rankings or Jiao Tong.

29. The normal requirement for a BA or BS at US universities is 120 semester-hours, and a semester is typically reckoned at 15-16 weeks, so total classroom hours are in the vicinity of 1800-2000.

30. The Higher Education system in England uses a unique credit system based on "notional hours of study," with a single humanities course lasting for a semester typically counting 15 credits – though many universities use a modular system in which each module or unit of study is double an ordinary 2–3 contact-hour class, and two of these 30-credit modules per semester (or two 20-credit modules per trimester) is considered a full course load. A 3-year BA program typically requires at least 360 total credits, of which no more than 60 are likely to be outside the major subject(s). For purposes of international transfer, a 15-credit class is generally

regarded as equivalent to a standard 3 hours per week semester-long class in the United States (3 credits) or to 6 standard European credits (called ECTS credits, after the European Credit Transfer and Accumulation System established by the Bologna process), though actual contact hours in Britain tend to be fewer. In all three systems, degree requirements would be based on the equivalent of 8–10 courses per year (if we regard a 6 ETCS, 3 hours per week half module in Europe as one course). For concise overviews of the credit systems in England and Europe, see Quality Assurance Agency for Higher Education, "Higher Education Credit Framework for England: Guidance on Academic Credit Arrangements in Higher Education in England" (Gloucester: Quality Assurance Agency for Higher Education, 2008), http://www.qaa.ac.uk; and World Education Services, "Understanding and Evaluating the 'Bologna Bachelor's Degree'" (New York: World Education Services, 2007), http://www.wes.org.

31. For example, *English through Culture: A Comprehensive Course Book for English Majors* (Beijing: Foreign Language Teaching and Research Press, 2009).

32. An example is the highly ranked Tsinghua University, where nearly 40% of the English majors are international students. That BA program includes courses entitled Western Society and Culture, British Culture, American History, and so on.

33. Fan Dai, "English Language Creative Writing in Mainland China," *World Englishes* 29 (2010): 546–549.

34. Yuanyuan Hu, "China's English Language Policy for Primary Schools," *World Englishes* 27.3–4 (2008): 516–534.

35. At Peking University, the English department has abolished the separate linguistics track at the undergraduate level due to insufficient student interest.

36. Mao Liang, personal communication, Peking University, May 2010.

37. In a recent survey of China's English departments, Junyue Chang notes the range of new "English Plus" formats and describes six basic models, only one of which (model 4) positions English as a service unit to other disciplines. Model 1 has English majors doing the regular curriculum in English plus courses in a range of other fields in order to broaden their education. This model is affecting all major subjects and marks a trend toward the liberal arts cur-

riculum in China. Model 2 has students completing the English major plus substantial coursework in one other discipline, but not enough to constitute a formal "minor" in that field. In model 3, that second discipline does constitute an official minor alongside the English major. In model 4, the student's major is in a different subject than English, but the student completes a substantial number of courses in English, typically in order to show English language proficiency when applying for jobs in business or the sciences. Model 5 is like models 2 and 3, the English major plus a second field of substantial study (possibly a minor), but the second field in this case is another foreign language. For careers in government and translation especially, trilinguality is regarded as a strong credential. Finally, model 6 is the double-major or dual-degree arrangement whereby a student completes all requirements for the English BA as well as for the BA in a second discipline. Junyue Chang, "Research Report: Globalization and English in Chinese Higher Education," *World Englishes* 2.3–4 (2006): 513–525.

38. Kayman, *Report of a Survey on English Studies in Europe*, 6.
39. Ina Habermann, personal correspondence, July 2011.
40. Kayman, *Report of a Survey on English Studies in Europe*, 6.
41. Kayman, *Report of a Survey on English Studies in Europe*, 3.
42. Rudolph Glitz, personal correspondence, 28 June 2011.
43. Jean Kempf, "American Studies in France: A Critical Review," *European Journal of American Studies* (2006): document 6.
44. Kempf, "American Studies in France."
45. Philipp Schweighauser, "Literature and Other Media: What Are They Made Of?" Syllabus for a seminar at the University of Basel, spring 2010.
46. Thus, for example, at the University of Amsterdam there is a 2-year MA program in cultural analysis, with faculty drawn from art history, film studies, urban studies, and literature.
47. I have discussed this in James English, "Everywhere and Nowhere: The Sociology of Literature after 'the Sociology of Literature,'" in "New Sociologies of Literature," ed. James F. English and Rita Felski, a special issue of *New Literary History* 41.2 (Spring 2010): v–xxiii.
48. Antony Easthope, *Literary into Cultural Studies* (New York: Routledge, 1991), 5.

49. In one of the widely circulating jeremiads of that period, Roger Kimball decried the "effort to *academicize* popular culture" as a "radical chic" trend that developed in the 1960s and that, by the late 1980s, had "become commonplace in the academy, where the degraded and demotic world of pop culture has been embraced wholesale." Roger Kimball, *Tenured Radicals: How Politics Has Corrupted Our Higher Education* (Chicago: Ivan R. Dee, 1991), 81. One could cite dozens of more or less identical diatribes.

50. Art Spiegelman, *Maus: A Survivor's Tale*, 25th anniversary ed. (New York: Pantheon, 1996).

51. According to a widely publicized NEA report, the percentage of persons age 18–24 who had read even a little bit of literature in the previous year fell from 60% in 1982 to 53% in 1992 and 43% in 2002. National Endowment for the Arts, *Reading at Risk: A Survey of Literary Reading in America*, Research Division Report No. 46, June (Washington, DC: NEA, 2004). A range of responses to the report from English professors are gathered in *Forum: A Journal of the Association of Literary Scholars and Critics* 2 (Spring 2005). As a number of these respondents point out, the survey data sketch a very rough and potentially misleading story. In particular, the statistics regarding college students and college graduates need to be viewed in light of the massification of higher education. For example, while literary reading among college graduates fell from 83% in 1982 to 67% in 2002, the latter figure is referring to such a broader swath of the US population that in absolute terms the number of such college-educated readers actually rose 50%, from 24 million to 36 million. Nevertheless, I stand by my point that English studies should be more aggressively extending its scholarly and curricular engagements with popular nonprint media.

52. As Simone Murray details in her fine recent study, the fact that "fidelity criticism has been able to maintain such an obdurate hold" over adaptation studies is partly owing to certain marketing strategies of the literary adaptation industry itself; Simone Murray, *The Adaptation Industry: The Cultural Economy of Contemporary Literary Adaptation* (New York: Routledge, 2011), 27. Her work, like that of others at the forefront of the field, abandons the outmoded habit of "privileging a specific subset of print texts" as the great originals whose genius it is the task of the adaptating director to preserve in the new, lesser medium. What is now emerging is a quite dif-

ferent conception of adaptation as a "freewheeling cultural process . . . more weblike than straightforwardly linear in its creative dynamic," and irreducible to any hierarchical cultural binary such as original–copy or literature–film (2). This does not at all mean that the novel should drop away from courses on adaptation, only that English studies should be capable of doing more in such a flourishing and pedagogically vibrant field than conducting rearguard exercises in fidelity criticism.

53. The only scholarly study of audiobooks that I'm aware of is the recent collection edited by Matthew Rubery, *Audiobooks, Literature, and Sound Studies* (New York: Routledge, 2011).

54. Geraldine Heng, whom I quote here, is one of the few literary scholars outside Australia who has acknowledged that to move the discipline forward and establish "twenty-first-century alliances," we may need to "edge past our current knowledge construction boundaries to make common-cause collaborations further afield – say, with the dreaded quantitative social sciences, with their fidelities to data collection and empiricism." The goal, as she nicely expresses it, would be "mashups of qualitative and quantitative, multilayered modes of inquiry – microreading and macroreading performed as a single dance." Geraldine Heng, "Holy War Redux: The Crusades, Futures of the Past, and Strategic Logic in the Clash of Religions," *PMLA* 126.2 (March 2011): 428.

55. On the material text in the digital age, for example, there is Matthew G. Kirschenbaum's superb *Mechanisms: New Media and the Forensic Imagination* (Cambridge, MA: MIT, 2008). Quantitative analysis has long been part of book-historical studies, but was kicked into a high gear of methodological innovation with the intervention of Franco Moretti's *Graphs, Maps, Trees: Abstract Models for a Literary History* (London: Verso 2005). Since then there have been a number of parallel projects involving the visual presentation of quantitative information gleaned from massive searchable datasets – most notably, perhaps, the Victorian Books project of Dan Cohen and Fred Gibbs (see http://www.victorianbooks.org).

56. For an alarmist account of the abandonment of the Great Authors requirement by US English departments, see "The Shakespeare File: What American English Majors Are Really Studying," a 1996 report by the American Council of Trustees and Alumni (ACTA), revised and updated as *The Vanishing Shakespeare* in 2007 (both

available online at http://www.goacta.org). This shoddy report is typical of propaganda from the right wing of the 1990s culture wars. ACTA was first launched, as the National Alumni Forum, by Lynne Cheney, infamous chair of the National Endowment for the Humanities for Bush I and wife of Dick Cheney, infamous warmonger and vice president for Bush II. The organization's remit is to increase the control of the Boards of Governors and Trustees (i.e., wealthy, powerful, non-academics) over curricular matters at American universities. Like most academics, the ACTA favors a broad liberal arts education, but it can only imagine achieving its goals by imposing, via governing boards, ever more requirements on students and faculties. And at the level of individual disciplines, the ACTA's agenda is predictably trapped in amber.

57.   At least this was the case at the time of the Millennial Survey conducted by Kayman *et al.*

58.   It is not, of course, only English programs that have undergone this tilt in Australian universities toward co-accommodation of multiple cultural forms and media. Peter Morgan describes a "dramatic" reconfiguration of Australia's programs in "European 'languages and literature,'" which have at least since the 1980s been "developing broadly 'cultural'-based courses in which communicative competence in language is bolstered through the study of popular culture, social studies, and film, alongside literary texts." Peter Morgan, "Europe from Down Under: A Case Study in the Development of European Studies Programmes outside Europe," *Journal of Education Studies* 29 (1999): 79–95.

59.   Programs bearing the name "cultural studies" are abundant enough in other national systems, but the vast majority are essentially social sciences programs in area studies or international studies, with few if any elements of British-style "critical" cultural studies and no discernible links to the latter's literary roots.

60.   A good overview of the post-1988 higher educational sector is Simon Marginson and Mark Considine, *The Enterprise University: Power, Governance and Reinvention in Australia* (Cambridge: Cambridge University Press, 2000).

61.   According to the Australian Research Council, faculty in literary studies account for 365 of the 1610 FTEs in "Language, Communication, and Culture," while faculty in cultural studies account for 380. Australian Research Council, *Excellence in*

184

Research for Australia, 2010 National Report (Canberra: ARC, 2010), 15.

62. Nationwide, BA enrollments in "communications and media studies" are about a third more than in "language and literature," and have been growing over the last 5 years at 3–4% per year, versus 1.5–2.0% per year for literature.

63. A 2006 piece by Rosemary Neill in the conservative newspaper *The Australian* kicked off a nationwide debate over the neglect of Australian literature in the higher educational system, which Neill attributed mainly to "colonial cringing" on the part of the country's English professors. The furor led to a national study of the "Oz Lit" curriculum at the secondary and tertiary levels. Of course, Neill's conservative readers understand "Australian" literature to mean the work of white authors, not of indigenous ones. See Rosemary Neill, "Lost for Words," *The Weekend Australian Review* 2–3 December 2006, 4–6; and Jill Rowbotham, "Oz Lit Teaching in the Spotlight," *The Australian*, 2 April 2008, http://www.theaustralian.news.com.au/story/0,25197,23468231-12332,00.html.

64. I am offering here no more than an updated and transnational version of the argument made most authoritatively by Gerald Graff back during the culture wars: that the supposed gutting of the core literary curriculum in English was largely a myth. Gerald Graff, "The Vanishing Classics and Other Myths: Two Episodes in the Culture War," in Graff, *Beyond the Culture Wars: How Teaching the Conflicts Can Revitalize American Education* (New York: Norton, 1992), 16–36.

65. Mark McGurl, *The Program Era: Postwar Fiction and the Rise of Creative Writing* (Cambridge, MA: Harvard University Press, 2009).

66. There are in fact a number of PhD programs in English or comparative literature that permit a creative thesis (which in some cases would be a work of translation). But while there are at least 100 such "Creative Writing Ph.D. programs" officially listed by universities in the United States, Australia, and the United Kingdom, many of them appear to be without students.

67. This is certainly an undercount of creative writing concentrators, however. The NCES statistics are limited by what is actually tabulated and reported by colleges and universities. By and large, the data cannot distinguish an English BA recipient with concentration in creative writing from one with concentration in, say, American

literature. NCES, *Digest of Education Statistics* 2010, Table 286: "Bachelor's, Master's, and Doctor's Degrees Conferred by Degree-Granting Institutions, by Sex of Student and Discipline Division: 2008–09."

68. These figures were tabulated by the Association of Writers & Writing Programs and published online in the *AWP Official Guide to Writing Programs*, http://guide.awpwriter.org. The AWP database probably undercounts creative writing programs at every level; Seth Abramson has compiled a list with almost twice as many screenwriting-scriptwriting MFA programs, for example, and half again as many low-residency MFA programs. See Abramson's blog at http://sethabramson.blogspot.com.

69. As mentioned in the discussion of US enrollments in Part I of this book, the subcategory of "Visual and Performing Arts" has been the fastest growing within the broad humanities category as tracked by NCES.

70. Nick Everett, "Creative Writing and English," *Cambridge Quarterly* 34.3 (2005): 232.

71. John Dale, "The Rise and Rise of Creative Writing," *The Conversation* 25 May 2011. Dale reports that, according to the national government's 2010 Excellence in Research Assessment (ERA), creative writing "produced twice as many research outputs" as literary studies. This is not really the case, since the outputs reported for creative writing are lumped together with those for music, drama, and performance studies; presumably the total for creative writing alone would be significantly less. One might also question what exactly the Research Council is counting when they count "non-traditional research outputs." Nearly three quarters of the "Performing Arts and Creative Writing" research outputs fall into this anything-at-all category, while the number of outputs classified as books, book chapters, and journal articles is tiny compared with the research outputs of literary studies. Australian Research Council, *Excellence in Research for Australia, 2010 National Report* (Canberra: ARC, 2010), 182, 188.

72. This was Barrett Wendell's course in Advanced Composition in the 1880s. See David Gershom Myers, *The Elephants Teach: Creative Writing since 1880* (New York: Prentice-Hall, 1995).

73. A selectivity ranking of creative writing programs has been compiled by Seth Abramson at http://sethabramson.blogspot.com. It

shows that Vanderbilt led the way with a .97% acceptance rate in 2010 (6 out of 620 applicants). The 3.2% acceptance rate at Harvard Medical School would not rank it even among the top 20 creative writing programs. Yale Law School at 7.7%, and Stanford GSB at 9%, would not make the top 50. The top MFA programs in the United States, much like the leading PhD programs, provide fellowships to cover students' tuition and living expenses. Outside the United States, where MFA students generally pay full tuition, the programs are not nearly as selective.

74. Based on requirements as stated on program and department websites as of July 2011. The courses, credits, and modules at East Anglia and Nottingham are set up differently from those in the US programs, but the programs' websites specify that three quarters of the curriculum at East Anglia and two thirds of it at Nottingham must be devoted to literary study.

75. If the language and composition quotient here looks low, that is because at many American universities the freshman composition class and any other general requirements in language arts, along with developmental writing classes and the like, are not accepted as credits toward the English major. These would therefore be included among the classes in "other departments."

76. For example, Steven Lynn invokes Wendell among the founding figures in *Rhetoric and Composition: An Introduction* (Cambridge: Cambridge University Press, 2010), 21. Wendell is not uncontroversial in the field, however. For the long list of criticisms that have been leveled at him and his pedagogical theories, see Thomas Newkirk, "Barrett Wendell's Theory of Discourse," *Rhetoric Review* 10.1 (1991): 20–30.

77. This being the Leavisite rationale for English as it was widely exported and successfully glocalized from the 1950s to the 1980s.

78. Richard Caves, *Creative Industries: Contracts between Art and Commerce* (Cambridge, MA: Harvard University Press, 2000).

79. Richard Florida, *The Rise of the Creative Class, and How It's Transforming Work, Leisure, and Everyday Life* (New York: Basic Books, 2002).

80. Quotations and curricular requirements taken from the department and school websites: see http://www.bathspa.ac.uk. Further information regarding student preferences for single or joint Honours

and for elective modules were found in the "Bath Spa Creative Writing 2009–2010" Facebook page.

81. David Milch, in a response to my questions at an event at Kelly Writers House, Philadelphia, April 2010.

82. In a radio interview with Terry Gross, the largely self-taught novelist Donald Ray Pollock (*Knockenstiff, The Devil All the Time*) said he learned to write in just this way, by copying out the stories he really admired from start to finish. "David Ray Pollock on Finding Fiction Late in Life," *Fresh Air*, National Public Radio, 26 July 2011.

83. The averages shown on this chart, based on bits of empirical data cobbled together from heterogeneous sources, are obviously very roughly estimated, and I offer them only as ballpark indicators. A couple of points may require explanation. First, the "language" category, which includes basic composition and other language arts and skills classes, may look to be grossly underestimated for US English majors. But while students do typically take more than one class in this category, that coursework is often not countable toward the major. Rather, it fulfills general university requirements which must be met by students in all majors. In many English departments, zero courses of this kind may be counted toward the major – even if they are taught in the English department. Second, for American English majors I have estimated an average of two classes in creative writing. This assumes that about 10–15% of reported majors are either on a creative writing track or maximizing their creative writing course load, and that creative writing is now a large enough presence at undergraduate level that about half of all English majors take a creative writing class even if they are not concentrators in that field. In Australia, where creative writing has a more vocational cast and is situated at greater institutional remove from English, and where bachelor's-level creative writing tracks are less common than MA programs, I have estimated one class in the field averaged out across all reported English majors. For the United Kingdom, I am estimating that creative writing is still, on average, too small a fraction of the English BA programs nationwide to register on our chart. That estimate may be in arrears of the reality, which is clearly trending toward more creative writing.

MANIFESTO

Is there any more shopworn, tedious, and plainly self-defeating story of our discipline than the crisis narrative? Isn't everybody tired of hearing about the death of English studies, the killing of Shakespeare, the last of the literature professors? If you were young and looking for a subject to focus on in college, would you choose the one whose faculty were pronouncing it a fossil, a relic, a dinosaur discipline whose days of greatness are long past? Let's try an experiment: let's try for a while to live without the crisis narrative. Let's try to tell some new stories, stories that don't lean on the keywords *crisis*, *death*, and *decline*: stories about our discipline's future as a durable and adaptable fixture on the expanding landscape of global higher education.

Enrollments. The future of higher education is one in which students around the world, forced to pay more for their degrees, claim greater freedom to choose their curriculum. The time is fast coming to an end when an exam at age 17 decides which subject will be your exclusive field of study. Already more and more students are finding their way to a major after matriculation, and to a second major, a minor, a majorless triple minor, an individuated interdisciplinary program, or the like. Students will increasingly

The Global Future of English Studies, First Edition. James F. English.
© 2012 John Wiley & Sons, Ltd. Published 2012 by John Wiley & Sons, Ltd.

take off years, return later in life, enroll part-time, study at more than one institution, and take their degrees abroad. English studies holds many advantages on this kind of terrain: its uncontested nodal position in the humanities; its hospitality to modular and interdisciplinary degree tracks; its lead role in fostering faculty diversity; its increasing accommodation of creative work; its particular ethical commitment to teaching and mentorship; its unique ability to offer higher credentials in the global lingua franca; its common core curriculum around the world; its foundational interest not just in the modern classics but also in the most vital culture of the contemporary moment. Academe is not the small world it's cracked up to be; comprehensive universities offer more than 50 undergraduate major programs, and hundreds of different ways to combine them. English studies is just one player on this vast and busy field. But it is positioned as a natural winner.

Faculty. Explaining that faculty in English are overworked, underpaid, and stressed by insecurity hasn't gotten us very far with a public that mostly faces lower salaries and less security than we do. Nor has it deterred our paymasters from further degrading the conditions of our labor. The story we need to be spreading is not about our unmet needs and desires but about the quality of students' educational experience. It is students who stand to lose the most from the over-reliance on throw-away instructors. Casualization of the instructional workforce makes an academic unit, including its diminished tenured component, demonstrably less effective in every aspect of its teaching, advising, and administration. Beyond a point, it more or less guarantees dysfunction. This is what students, parents, and university ranking services need to hear. The universities and the state and national systems that are leading the trend toward contingency (notably those in the United States and South America) need to understand that they are entering a highly competitive global market in which their degree programs will increasingly be recognized as shoddy and overpriced. The most effective pushback against casualization will be that which comes from the consumer side of the higher educational system.

Curriculum. The future expansion of English studies will mostly occur outside the discipline's traditional Anglophone and European base. We are approaching a turning point at which, in strictly quantitative terms, the most consequential decisions about what and how we teach will be made on the seeming peripheries of the discipline. This represents an opportunity for all of us in the field to unsettle the established pattern of time-lag emulation, whereby the literary curriculum at a university in Seoul resembles that of a university in New York 30 years earlier. The tail of foreign variants is becoming long enough to wag the dog of domestic English lit. The English departments in East Asia, only just now beginning to test the water of Anglophone Asian literatures, could have much to contribute to the future of that burgeoning field. The leading departments in South Africa and Nigeria can and should be looked to for a new, less London-oriented syllabus in postcolonial African literature. The departments in Brazil and Mexico can help to shape a new canon of American literatures and to develop the new models we require for a bi- or trilingual American literary studies. Just as important will be the ways that English, in these supposedly secondary locations, comes to be positioned relative to other disciplines: language and linguistics, film and media, communications and journalism, sociology and area studies, creative and performing arts, and so on. History has shown that the sudden expansion of an educational system, with the founding of many new universities, tends to produce new clusterings of faculties and departments, new degree options, new tracks and concentrations. It is time for those of us at the presumptive center of things to begin paying more attention to the forms our discipline is taking at these sites of rapid expansion. As an ever more global discipline, English studies is going to find that some of its best pathways for the future lie far from its traditional homes.

Index

The Global Future of English Studies, First Edition. James F. English.
© 2012 John Wiley & Sons, Ltd. Published 2012 by John Wiley & Sons, Ltd.